How to Make leather Shoe

Shelly Norris

Published by CEC Publisher, 2024.

This is a work of fiction. Similarities to real people, places, or events are entirely coincidental.

HOW TO MAKE LEATHER SHOE

First edition. March 10, 2024.

Written by Shelly Norris.

Table of Contents

How to Make leather Shoe

The Simple Guide to Learning Best Technique
About How to Make leather Shoe

Shelly Norris

Disclaimer

While every precaution has been taken in the preparation of this book, the publisher assumes no responsibility for errors or omissions, or for damages resulting from the use of the information contained herein.

How to Make leather Shoe: The Simple Guide to Learning Best Technique About How to Make leather Shoe

First edition.

Table of Contents

Chapter 4

Mastering Patterns and Templates

Creating Basic Patterns

Patterns for Different Shoe Types

Scaling Patterns for Custom Sizing

Adjusting Patterns for Individual Feet

As we embark on this journey of adjusting patterns for individual feet, this guide becomes an essential companion for shoemakers committed to crafting footwear that transcends the boundaries of standard sizing. "Adjusting Patterns for Individual Feet" not only demystifies the intricacies of customization but also celebrates the union of art and science in creating shoes that are not just worn but truly experienced.

Chapter 5

The Craft of Cutting and Stitching
Precision Cutting Techniques
Tips for Accurate Cutting
Stitching Methods
Hand Stitching vs. Machine Stitching

Chapter 6

Lasting and Assembling

Understanding Lasts

Choosing the Right Last for Your Design

Embark on a journey where design aspirations meet the precision of last selection. "Choosing the Right Last for Your Design" is more than a guide; it is your companion in sculpting footwear that transcends trends, standing as a testament to the harmonious fusion of artistry and functionality. May your design journey be as rewarding as the steps you take in crafting the perfect fit.

Techniques for Lasting and Attaching Soles

Chapter 7

Finishing Touches
Sanding and Buffing
Polishing and Coloring
Enhancing the Aesthetic Appeal

Chapter 8

Troubleshooting and Quality Control

Common Issues in Shoemaking

Solutions to Potential Problems

Quality Control Measures

Embark on a journey through the world of quality control, where excellence is not just a goal but a commitment. "Ensuring Excellence: A Comprehensive Guide to Quality Control Measures" is your companion in navigating the intricacies of maintaining high standards across diverse industries. From principles and methodologies to real-world applications, this guide empowers professionals and enthusiasts alike to champion quality in their respective domains. May this exploration inspire a renewed dedication to excellence and continuous improvement.

Ensuring Every Shoe Meets Standards

Embark on a comprehensive exploration of the rigorous processes, uncompromising standards, and innovative approaches that define quality assurance in the world of shoemaking. "Ensuring Every Shoe Meets Standards" is not just a guide; it's an immersive journey into the heart of an industry dedicated to the pursuit of excellence—one step at a time. Whether you're a seasoned professional or an enthusiast, this guide promises a deeper understanding of the intricate processes that transform raw materials into footwear that stands the test of time. Welcome to the realm where craftsmanship, precision, and passion converge to ensure that every shoe meets and exceeds the highest standards.

Chapter 9

Exploring Advanced Techniques

Incorporating Unique Design Elements

Embark on a captivating journey through the world of shoemaking, where each step is a brushstroke on the canvas of uniqueness. "Incorporating Unique Design Elements" is not merely a guide; it's an ode to the creative spirit that propels shoemakers to push boundaries and redefine the very essence of footwear. Whether you're a seasoned designer or an enthusiast, this guide promises a profound understanding of the artistry that transforms shoes into wearable masterpieces, each telling a story as unique as the person who wears them. Welcome to a universe where every step is a statement—a testament to the seamless fusion of innovation, aesthetics, and the indomitable spirit of creativity.

Experimental Techniques in Shoemaking

Embark on a thrilling exploration of experimental shoemaking, where every pair becomes a testament to innovation, creativity, and a commitment to pushing boundaries. "Experimental Techniques in Shoemaking" is not just a book; it's an invitation to witness the convergence of tradition and futuristic vision. Whether you're a seasoned shoemaker, a design enthusiast, or someone seeking insight into the evolution of footwear, this guide promises a captivating journey through the uncharted territories of experimental shoemaking. Welcome to a world where every step is an expression, and every shoe is a work of art in motion.

Pushing the Boundaries of Innovation

Innovation isn't a solitary pursuit; it's a collective force that shapes the future. "Pushing the Boundaries of Innovation in Modern Industry" is not just a documentation of progress; it's an invitation to envision the limitless potential that unfolds when creativity meets determination. Whether you're an entrepreneur, a business leader, or an enthusiast of the ever-evolving landscape of innovation, this exploration promises an insightful journey into the heart of transformative change. Welcome to a world where each idea is a spark, and each innovation is a step into the uncharted territories of possibility.

Future Trends in Shoemaking

Conclusion

Foreword

IN THE VAST LANDSCAPE of self-improvement literature, "How to Make a Shoe" stands out as a beacon of craftsmanship and innovation. This book transcends the ordinary and delves into the artistry and precision required to create footwear that not only graces our feet but tells a story of meticulous design and passion.

As we embark on this journey with the author, we are guided through the intricate process of shoemaking, from the selection of materials to the final stitch. What sets this guide apart is its commitment to demystifying the seemingly complex world of cobbling, making it accessible to both novices and seasoned artisans.

The author's expertise and love for the craft shine through every page, offering not just a manual but an immersive experience. Whether you aspire to launch your own shoe line or simply wish to deepen your appreciation for the art of shoemaking, this book serves as an indispensable companion.

Prepare to be inspired, educated, and captivated by the wisdom shared within these pages. "How to Make a Shoe" isn't just a guide—it's a testament to the beauty found in the union of skill, creativity, and dedication. May your journey in shoemaking be as enriching as the one you are about to embark upon within these transformative chapters.

Chapter 1

Understanding the Art of Shoemaking

The History and Evolution of Shoemaking

The History and Evolution of Shoemaking: A Journey Through Time

Shoemaking, an ancient craft that has left its imprint on the sands of time, weaves a narrative of human ingenuity and the quest for both practicality and artistry. In this exploration of the history and evolution of shoemaking, we embark on a fascinating journey that unveils the footsteps of civilizations, revealing how footwear has transcended mere necessity to become a testament to culture, craftsmanship, and innovation.

I. Inception of Footwear: Unearthing Ancient Origins

1.1. Primitive Foot Coverings: Tracing the earliest forms of foot protection in prehistoric times, from simple wrappings to rudimentary sandals.

1.2. Cultural Significance: Examining the symbolic role of early footwear in various ancient societies, where shoes became expressions of status, identity, and ritual.

II. Ancient Civilizations: Footwear as Art and Utility

2.1. Egyptian Elegance: Unveiling the sophistication of footwear in ancient Egypt, where craftsmanship and materials reflected social hierarchy.

2.2. Roman Innovations: Exploring the Roman Empire's contributions to shoemaking, from the practical caligae of soldiers to the opulent sandals worn by elites.

III. Medieval Mastery: Guilds, Craftsmen, and Renaissance

3.1. Guilds and Cobblers: Investigating the rise of shoemaking guilds in medieval Europe, where skilled craftsmen honed their expertise and passed down traditions.

3.2. Renaissance Revival: Examining the revival of footwear design during the Renaissance, marked by intricate patterns, luxurious materials, and a resurgence of fashion.

IV. Industrial Revolution: From Handcraft to Mass Production

4.1. Mechanization of Shoemaking: Charting the transformative impact of the Industrial Revolution on footwear production, leading to mass manufacturing and accessibility.

4.2. Innovations in Materials: Exploring the introduction of new materials, such as rubber and synthetic fabrics, revolutionizing the comfort and durability of shoes.

V. 20th Century and Beyond: Fashion, Technology, and Globalization

5.1. Fashion Footprints: Analyzing the evolution of shoe styles in the 20th century, shaped by fashion movements, celebrity culture, and changing societal norms.

5.2. Technological Advancements: Delving into how technology, from athletic shoe advancements to 3D printing, has propelled shoemaking into the 21st century.

VI. Cultural Impact: Shoes Beyond Utility

6.1. Shoes in Pop Culture: Investigating the cultural significance of iconic shoes in literature, film, and music, exploring their impact beyond the realm of fashion.

6.2. Sustainability and Ethical Shoemaking: Addressing the contemporary focus on sustainable practices and ethical considerations in the modern shoemaking industry.

As we traverse through the chapters of shoemaking history, it becomes evident that this journey is not just about footwear; it's a chronicle of human progress, creativity, and the intricate dance between form and function. "The History and Evolution of Shoemaking" invites readers to step into the past and appreciate how the simple act of covering our feet has shaped cultures, industries, and the very fabric of our shared history.

The Significance of Handcrafted Shoes

THE SIGNIFICANCE OF Handcrafted Shoes: Unveiling the Artistry Beneath Our Feet

In a world often dominated by mass production and fleeting trends, the significance of handcrafted shoes emerges as a beacon of timeless craftsmanship, individuality, and unrivaled quality. As we delve into the profound realm of artisanal shoemaking, we discover a narrative that transcends mere footwear; it is a story of passion, heritage, and the enduring allure of the handmade.

I. Embracing Tradition: The Legacy of Handcrafted Shoes

1.1. Historical Roots: Tracing the origins of handcrafted shoemaking, rooted in ancient traditions where skilled artisans crafted footwear tailored to individual needs.

1.2. Cultural Resonance: Exploring how handcrafted shoes have symbolized cultural identity, reflecting regional styles, materials, and techniques.

II. The Artisan's Touch: Craftsmanship and Techniques

2.1. Mastering the Craft: Unveiling the skills required for artisanal shoemaking, from pattern design and leather selection to precision stitching and lasting.

2.2. Unique Techniques: Highlighting specific artisanal techniques, such as hand welting and patina application, that elevate handcrafted shoes to wearable works of art.

III. Individuality in Every Stitch: Customization and Bespoke Shoemaking

3.1. Tailored Elegance: Exploring the world of bespoke shoemaking, where artisans create shoes uniquely fitted to an individual's foot shape and style preferences.

3.2. Personalized Details: Delving into the art of customization, from selecting exotic leathers to incorporating personalized touches like monograms and unique finishes.

IV. Quality Over Quantity: Materials and Ethical Considerations

4.1. Selecting Premium Materials: Discussing the importance of high-quality materials in handcrafted shoes, including fine leathers, exotic skins, and sustainable alternatives.

4.2. Ethical Shoemaking Practices: Examining the ethical considerations inherent in the artisanal approach, from fair labor practices to environmental sustainability.

V. The Enduring Appeal: Handcrafted Shoes in the Modern World

5.1. Luxury and Prestige: Analyzing the place of handcrafted shoes in the luxury market, where discerning consumers seek not just a product but an experience.

5.2. Artisanal Revival: Exploring the resurgence of interest in handmade products and the impact of the artisanal movement on the global fashion landscape.

VI. Beyond Fashion: Handcrafted Shoes as Heirlooms

6.1. Legacy and Heritage: Discussing how handcrafted shoes often become cherished family heirlooms, passed down through generations.

6.2. Appreciating the Craft: Encouraging a shift towards mindful consumerism, where individuals recognize the value of supporting artisans and investing in enduring quality.

As we navigate through the profound significance of handcrafted shoes, it becomes clear that these creations are not just articles of clothing; they are tangible expressions of human skill, culture, and the enduring pursuit of excellence. "The Significance of Handcrafted Shoes" invites readers to step into a world where each pair of shoes is a masterpiece, crafted with dedication, precision, and a profound appreciation for the art of shoemaking.

Chapter 2

Essential Tools and Materials

Selecting Quality Leather

Selecting Quality Leather: A Comprehensive Guide to Shoemakers' Gold

In the intricate realm of shoemaking, the choice of leather is akin to selecting the finest canvas for a masterpiece. The very essence of craftsmanship lies in the quality of materials, and when it comes to shoes, it all begins with the leather. In this comprehensive exploration, we unveil the art and science of selecting quality leather, delving into the diverse world of hides, finishes, and the meticulous considerations that transform raw material into the foundation of exceptional footwear.

I. Understanding Leather Basics: The Anatomy of Quality

1.1. Grades and Cuts: Navigating through the different grades of leather, from full-grain to corrected grain, and understanding how each cut impacts durability and aesthetics.

1.2. Tanning Methods: Exploring traditional and modern tanning processes, such as vegetable tanning and chrome tanning, and their influence on leather properties.

II. Types of Leather and Their Characteristics: Navigating the Landscape

2.1. Cowhide: A Staple for Durability: Investigating the most common leather type used in shoemaking, its durability, and how variations like steerhide and calfskin offer unique attributes.

2.2. Exotic Leathers: Unveiling the luxury of exotic options like alligator, ostrich, and snake, and understanding their distinctive textures, patterns, and considerations in use.

III. Factors Influencing Leather Quality: Beyond the Surface

3.1. Thickness Matters: Delving into the impact of leather thickness on shoe durability and comfort, and how shoemakers balance thickness for various styles.

3.2. Natural Characteristics: Understanding and appreciating the natural imperfections in leather, such as scars and wrinkles, as unique features that enhance character.

IV. Sustainable Leather Choices: Ethical Considerations

4.1. Environmental Impact: Discussing the ecological footprint of leather production and exploring sustainable practices, including vegetable-tanned and eco-friendly alternatives.

4.2. Ethical Sourcing: Examining the importance of responsible sourcing, fair labor practices, and certifications in ensuring the ethical production of leather.

V. Finishes and Treatments: Elevating Aesthetics and Functionality

5.1. Dyeing Techniques: Analyzing the art of leather dyeing, including aniline, semi-aniline, and pigmented dyes, and their impact on color vibrancy and longevity.

5.2. Protective Coatings: Exploring finishes like waxing and oiling that enhance water resistance and provide a patina over time, contributing to the unique character of the leather.

VI. Navigating the Market: Tips for Consumers and Shoemakers

6.1. Recognizing Quality: Offering practical advice on how consumers can identify and appreciate quality leather when shopping for footwear.

6.2. Communication with Suppliers: Guiding shoemakers on effective communication with leather suppliers, ensuring they receive materials aligned with their specific requirements.

As we immerse ourselves in the nuances of selecting quality leather, it becomes clear that this seemingly mundane choice is the cornerstone of exceptional shoemaking. "Selecting Quality Leather" serves not only as a guide for the seasoned artisan but as an enlightening journey for anyone eager to grasp the essence of craftsmanship—one carefully selected hide at a time.

Types of Leather and Their Characteristics

TYPES OF LEATHER AND Their Characteristics: Decoding the Language of Hides

In the intricate world of leather, each type tells a story through its unique texture, durability, and aesthetic qualities. As we embark on this journey to understand the various types of leather, we unravel the rich tapestry of hides that have been a timeless companion in the crafting of shoes, garments, and accessories. From the robustness of cowhide to the exotic allure of reptilian skins, we delve into the characteristics that define each type, empowering enthusiasts and artisans alike to make informed choices in the world of leather craftsmanship.

I. Cowhide: The Backbone of Leather Craftsmanship

1.1. Full-Grain Cowhide: Unveiling the top-tier choice with its natural grain intact, showcasing strength, durability, and a character that matures with age.

1.2. Top-Grain Cowhide: Exploring the refined version with the outer layer sanded for a smoother finish, balancing durability with a more uniform appearance.

II. Calfskin: A Symphony of Elegance and Softness

2.1. Veal Calfskin: Investigating the delicate and luxurious veal calfskin, known for its fine grain and supple texture, making it a favorite for upscale footwear.

2.2. Full-Grain Calfskin: Examining how full-grain calfskin combines softness with durability, providing an exquisite choice for dress shoes and accessories.

III. Exotic Leathers: Unraveling the Extraordinary

3.1. Alligator and Crocodile: Delving into the world of luxury with the distinctive scales of alligator and crocodile leather, exploring their durability and opulent appeal.

3.2. Ostrich Leather: Analyzing the unique quill patterns of ostrich leather, prized for its softness, flexibility, and striking visual impact in luxury products.

IV. Sheepskin: The Pinnacle of Softness

4.1. Lambskin: Exploring the unmatched softness and lightweight nature of lambskin, a popular choice for fine garments and delicate accessories.

4.2. Shearling: Examining the natural insulation and plush texture of shearling, often used in the lining of boots and cold-weather accessories.

V. Goat Leather: A Balance of Strength and Suppleness

5.1. Kid and Full-Grain Goat Leather: Investigating the durable yet flexible nature of goat leather, renowned for its weather resistance and versatility.

5.2. Suede and Nubuck: Exploring the velvety textures of suede and nubuck, created from the grain side of goat leather, offering a luxurious feel.

VI. Pigskin: The Durable Underdog

6.1. Benefits of Pigskin: Highlighting the surprisingly durable and breathable qualities of pigskin, often utilized in casual footwear and sportswear.

6.2. Suede and Split Pigskin: Examining the applications of pigskin suede and split pigskin in various products, from gloves to upholstery.

As we navigate the diverse landscape of leather, each type beckons with its own allure and purpose. "Types of Leather and Their Characteristics" serves as a comprehensive guide, empowering both seasoned artisans and curious enthusiasts to appreciate the nuances of each hide, ultimately making informed choices that elevate the art of leather craftsmanship.

Tools of the Trade

TOOLS OF THE TRADE: Crafting Excellence with Precision Instruments

In the realm of shoemaking, the journey from raw materials to a refined pair of shoes involves a symphony of meticulous steps, and at the heart of this craftsmanship lies an array of essential tools. This exploration delves into the tools of the trade, unveiling the precision instruments that transform leather into wearable art. From cutting and stitching to lasting and assembling, each tool plays a vital role in the hands of skilled artisans, creating a harmonious dance of craftsmanship and functionality.

I. Cutting Tools: Precision from the First Stroke

1.1. Skiving Knife: Unveiling the versatile skiving knife, an indispensable tool for thinning leather edges and achieving seamless joins.

1.2. Clicker Die: Exploring the efficiency of clicker dies in mass production, providing consistent and precise shapes for various shoe components.

II. Stitching Instruments: Thread by Thread Mastery

2.1. Awl and Brad: Navigating the usage of the awl and brad for puncturing precise holes, a crucial step in hand-stitching intricate designs.

2.2. Sewing Machine: Analyzing the role of modern sewing machines in enhancing efficiency while maintaining the durability of hand-stitched footwear.

III. Lasting Tools: Shaping the Foundation

3.1. Lasting Pliers: Examining the ergonomic design of lasting pliers, essential for securing the upper to the shoe last with precision.

3.2. Crimping Iron: Uncovering the crimping iron's role in shaping leather over the shoe last, ensuring a snug fit and refined aesthetics.

IV. Assembling Equipment: Bringing Components Together

4.1. Hammer and Nails: Investigating the timeless combination of hammer and nails for attaching soles securely, a fundamental step in shoemaking.

4.2. Adhesives and Cement: Exploring modern adhesives and cement, offering efficient alternatives for joining components with precision and durability.

V. Edge Finishing Tools: Refining the Details

5.1. Edge Beveler: Delving into the use of edge bevelers to round and smooth raw leather edges, adding a polished and professional finish.

5.2. Burnishing Tools: Analyzing burnishing tools for creating a glossy edge, enhancing both the aesthetics and longevity of the finished shoe.

VI. Specialty Tools: Elevating Craftsmanship

6.1. Lasting Machine: Discussing the role of lasting machines in large-scale production, streamlining the lasting process with consistent results.

6.2. Pattern Cutting Software: Exploring the integration of technology with pattern cutting software, providing precision and customization in design.

As we journey through the tools of the trade, it becomes evident that each instrument is not just an inanimate object but an extension of the artisan's skill and vision. "Tools of the Trade" seeks to illuminate the craft, offering insights into the significance of these precision instruments, and inspiring both aspiring and seasoned shoemakers to wield them with mastery, creating footwear that transcends functionality to become wearable works of art.

Must-Have Tools for Shoemakers

MUST-HAVE TOOLS FOR Shoemakers: A Symphony of Craftsmanship

In the world of shoemaking, the journey from raw materials to a finely crafted pair of shoes is an intricate dance that requires precision, skill, and a carefully curated set of tools. As we embark on this exploration of must-have tools for shoemakers, we unravel the secrets behind the artistry—tools that transform leather into wearable masterpieces. From the initial stages of pattern cutting to the final touches of polishing, each instrument is a silent protagonist in the creation of footwear that transcends mere utility to become a testament to the craftsman's expertise.

I. Cutting Tools: Crafting the Canvas

1.1. Utility Knife: Unveiling the versatility of the utility knife, a staple in cutting leather with precision and efficiency.

1.2. Rotary Cutter: Exploring the rotary cutter's role in pattern cutting, providing clean and accurate lines for intricate designs.

1.3. Strap Cutter: Navigating the usage of strap cutters for creating consistent and evenly sized leather strips, crucial for various shoe components.

II. Stitching Instruments: Binding the Threads of Craftsmanship

2.1. Awl Set: Analyzing the essential awl set, indispensable for creating precise holes and guiding stitches through multiple layers of leather.

2.2. Stitching Horse: Delving into the utility of the stitching horse, a tool that secures the shoe in place, allowing the artisan to focus on meticulous stitching.

2.3. Wax Thread and Needles: Exploring the significance of high-quality waxed thread and specialized needles in ensuring durable and aesthetically pleasing stitches.

III. Lasting Tools: Shaping the Foundation

3.1. Lasting Pliers: Investigating the ergonomic design and usage of lasting pliers, essential for securing the upper to the shoe last with precision.

3.2. Crimping Iron: Uncovering the crimping iron's role in shaping leather over the shoe last, ensuring a snug fit and refined aesthetics.

3.3. Steam Machine: Analyzing the importance of steam machines in softening and molding leather during the lasting process.

IV. Finishing Tools: Elevating the Aesthetics

4.1. Edge Beveler: Delving into the use of edge bevelers for rounding and smoothing raw leather edges, adding a polished and professional finish.

4.2. Burnishing Tools: Exploring burnishing tools for creating a glossy edge, enhancing both the aesthetics and longevity of the finished shoe.

4.3. Polishing Brushes: Discussing the role of polishing brushes in achieving a lustrous shine, the final touch that brings the shoes to life.

V. Specialty Tools: Precision Beyond the Basics

5.1. Lasting Machine: Investigating the role of lasting machines in large-scale production, streamlining the lasting process with consistent results.

5.2. Pattern Cutting Software: Exploring the integration of technology with pattern cutting software, providing precision and customization in design.

5.3. Shoemaker's Hammer: Analyzing the different types of hammers used in shoemaking, from tack hammers to lasting hammers, each serving a specific purpose.

As we navigate through the must-have tools for shoemakers, it becomes evident that these instruments are not just objects; they are extensions of the artisan's vision and expertise. "Must-Have Tools for Shoemakers" serves as a comprehensive guide, illuminating the significance of each tool and inspiring both aspiring and seasoned shoemakers to hone their craft with the precision and mastery these instruments demand.

Advanced Equipment for Precision

ADVANCED EQUIPMENT for Precision: Elevating Shoemaking to Artistry

In the ever-evolving world of shoemaking, precision is not just a goal; it's a pursuit of excellence that requires a harmonious blend of tradition and cutting-edge technology. As we delve into the realm of advanced equipment, we unveil the tools that transcend the boundaries of craftsmanship, elevating shoemaking to an art form. From computerized cutting systems to sophisticated 3D scanners, each piece of advanced equipment becomes a catalyst for precision, enabling artisans to push the boundaries of creativity while maintaining the meticulous standards that define exceptional footwear.

I. Automated Cutting Systems: Precision Beyond Measure

1.1. Computer Numerical Control (CNC) Cutting Machines: Unveiling the capabilities of CNC cutting machines that use computerized precision to cut intricate patterns with unparalleled accuracy.

1.2. Laser Cutting Technology: Exploring the application of laser cutting technology, allowing for the creation of intricate designs and complex patterns with minimal material waste.

II. 3D Scanning and Modeling: Crafting the Perfect Fit

2.1. 3D Scanners in Shoemaking: Navigating the usage of 3D scanners to capture precise measurements of a customer's foot, facilitating the creation of bespoke and perfectly fitting shoes.

2.2. Computer-Aided Design (CAD) Software: Delving into the role of CAD software in transforming 3D scans into detailed digital models, enabling virtual prototyping and customization.

III. Lasting Machines: A Symphony of Automation

3.1. Hydraulic Lasting Machines: Investigating the efficiency of hydraulic lasting machines that automate the lasting process, ensuring consistent results and reducing manual labor.

3.2. Toe-Lasting Machines: Exploring specialized machines designed for toe-lasting, a critical step in achieving the desired shape and appearance of the shoe.

IV. Computerized Sewing Machines: Stitching with Precision

4.1. Programmable Stitch Patterns: Analyzing the capabilities of computerized sewing machines that allow for programmable stitch patterns, ensuring uniformity and durability in every seam.

4.2. Automated Stitch Tension Control: Delving into the importance of automated stitch tension control, a feature that contributes to the overall quality and appearance of the finished product.

V. Last-Making Technology: Innovations in Form

5.1. 3D-Printed Lasts: Exploring the use of 3D printing technology in creating lasts, offering a level of customization and precision previously unattainable through traditional methods.

5.2. CNC Machined Lasts: Navigating the precision of CNC machining in crafting lasts, allowing for intricate details and modifications to accommodate diverse foot shapes.

VI. Advanced Finishing and Polishing Equipment: The Final Touch

6.1. Buffing and Polishing Machines: Investigating advanced machinery for buffing and polishing, ensuring a flawless finish and enhancing the visual appeal of the final product.

6.2. Automated Shoe Shining Devices: Exploring the integration of technology in shoe care with automated shoe shining devices, providing a convenient and efficient way to maintain the shine of finished shoes.

As we unravel the realm of advanced equipment for precision in shoemaking, it becomes evident that these tools are not just innovations; they are gateways to new possibilities. "Advanced Equipment for Precision" is a testament to the marriage of tradition and technology, where the artistry of shoemaking is enriched by the precision of cutting-edge equipment. This exploration invites both seasoned artisans and enthusiasts to embrace the future of shoemaking—a future where creativity knows no bounds, and precision is the cornerstone of excellence.

Chapter 3

Blueprint of a Shoe

Anatomy of a Shoe

Anatomy of a Shoe: Crafting the Soleful Symphony of Comfort and Style

In the realm of fashion and functionality, the anatomy of a shoe is a narrative that weaves together tradition, innovation, and the meticulous craftsmanship that transforms raw materials into wearable art. As we embark on this exploration of the intricate components that constitute the very essence of footwear, we unravel the secrets behind the structure, design, and engineering that define the anatomy of a shoe—each element contributing to a symphony of comfort and style that resonates with every step.

I. The Foundation: Understanding the Sole

1.1. Outsole: Unveiling the outsole as the protective layer that makes direct contact with the ground, exploring materials, and patterns for durability and traction.

1.2. Midsole: Navigating the midsole's role in providing cushioning and support, from traditional materials like leather to modern innovations such as EVA foam.

1.3. Insole: Delving into the insole's impact on comfort and arch support, exploring materials like leather, foam, and gel for personalized comfort.

II. The Upper: A Canvas of Expression

2.1. Toe Box: Analyzing the toe box's shape and materials, influencing the aesthetics and functionality of the shoe, from pointed to rounded designs.

2.2. Vamp: Exploring the vamp as the central part of the upper covering the instep, with variations in design, material, and closures.

2.3. Quarter and Heel Counter: Investigating the quarter's sides and the heel counter's reinforcement, enhancing stability and shape.

III. Fastenings: Securing Style and Fit

3.1. Laces: Unraveling the significance of laces in adjusting fit and adding a decorative element, exploring various lacing techniques and materials.

3.2. Buckles, Straps, and Zippers: Navigating alternative fastening methods, from the classic buckle to modern straps and zippers, influencing both aesthetics and functionality.

IV. Stitching and Construction: The Art of Assembly

4.1. Welt Construction: Analyzing the welt as a strip of material connecting the upper and sole, highlighting its role in durability and ease of repair.

4.2. Goodyear, Blake, and Cement Construction: Delving into different construction methods, their impact on flexibility, and the ease of resoling.

V. Comfort Innovations: Enhancing the Wear Experience

5.1. Orthopedic Features: Exploring orthopedic elements like arch support, metatarsal pads, and cushioned insoles for enhanced comfort and foot health.

5.2. Breathability and Moisture Management: Investigating technologies and materials that promote airflow, keeping feet dry and comfortable.

VI. Aesthetics and Branding: Beyond Functionality

6.1. Logo Placement and Branding: Analyzing how logos and branding contribute to the overall design, from discreet labels to prominent emblems.

6.2. Color and Material Combinations: Navigating the artistry of combining colors and materials, creating unique designs that reflect trends and individual style.

As we deconstruct the anatomy of a shoe, it becomes clear that each component is not merely a functional part but a piece of a carefully orchestrated ensemble. "Anatomy of a Shoe" invites readers into the world where tradition meets innovation, where design meets engineering, and where every element contributes to the creation of footwear that transcends utility to become a symbol of personal expression and timeless style.

Breaking Down Shoe Components

BREAKING DOWN SHOE Components: A Comprehensive Guide to the Heart of Footwear Design

In the intricate world of shoemaking, the beauty and functionality of a pair of shoes lie in the meticulous assembly of various components. As we embark on the journey of breaking down shoe components, we delve into the anatomy of footwear, unraveling the secrets behind each part that contributes to the comfort, style, and durability of the final product. From the sole to the upper, from fastenings to construction methods, this exploration is a testament to the craftsmanship that transforms raw materials into a wearable work of art.

I. The Foundation: Sole Construction and Materials

1.1. Outsole: Unveiling the outsole as the shoe's first line of defense, exploring materials like rubber, leather, and synthetic compounds for durability and traction.

1.2. Midsole and Insole: Navigating the layers beneath the foot, understanding how midsoles provide cushioning and insoles contribute to comfort and arch support.

1.3. Shank: Exploring the shank's role in supporting the arch, enhancing stability, and preventing excessive bending of the shoe.

II. The Canvas of Expression: The Upper and Its Components

2.1. Toe Box and Vamp: Analyzing the front of the upper, exploring toe box shapes, and understanding how the vamp covers the instep, influencing both aesthetics and functionality.

2.2. Quarter and Heel Counter: Investigating the sides of the upper, where the quarter meets the vamp, and understanding the importance of the heel counter in maintaining the shoe's shape.

III. Fastening Methods: Beyond Aesthetic Appeal

3.1. Laces and Eyelets: Delving into the various lacing systems, from classic crisscross patterns to innovative styles, and exploring the role of eyelets in securing the laces.

3.2. Buckles, Straps, and Zippers: Navigating alternative fastening methods, from the timeless buckle to modern straps and zippers, each influencing both aesthetics and functionality.

IV. Construction Techniques: The Art of Assembly

4.1. Welt Construction: Analyzing welted construction methods, understanding the role of the welt in connecting the upper and sole for durability and ease of repair.

4.2. Cement and Stitched Construction: Delving into different construction methods, such as cementing and stitching, and their impact on flexibility and resoling.

V. Comfort Enhancements: Beyond the Basics

5.1. Orthopedic Features: Exploring elements like arch support, cushioned insoles, and shock-absorbing technologies that enhance overall comfort and foot health.

5.2. Breathability and Moisture Management: Investigating innovations that promote airflow and moisture-wicking, ensuring a comfortable environment for the foot.

VI. Aesthetic Details: Elevating Design

6.1. Logo Placement and Branding: Analyzing how logos and branding contribute to the overall design, from discreet labels to prominent emblems.

6.2. Color and Material Combinations: Navigating the artistry of combining colors and materials, creating unique designs that reflect trends and individual style.

As we break down the myriad components that constitute a pair of shoes, it becomes clear that each part is not merely a functional element but a piece of a harmonious puzzle. "Breaking Down Shoe Components" serves as a comprehensive guide, offering insights into the craftsmanship and design principles that define quality footwear. This exploration invites both enthusiasts and seasoned shoemakers to appreciate the intricacies of shoe assembly, fostering a deeper understanding of the artistry that goes into creating the perfect pair.

Design Principles

DESIGN PRINCIPLES: Crafting Aesthetics and Functionality in Every Stitch

In the realm of fashion and footwear, the art of designing transcends the mere selection of colors and shapes. It is a harmonious blend of creativity, functionality, and an acute understanding of the human form. "Design Principles" is a voyage into the core of this artistry, exploring the fundamental elements and principles that guide the creation of exceptional and visually captivating footwear. From balance and proportion to color theory and innovation, this exploration illuminates the principles that transform raw materials into wearable masterpieces.

CONTENTS:

3.1. Balance and Symmetry: Investigating the role of balance and symmetry, from classic to avant-garde, and how these principles create visual harmony in shoe design.

3.2. Proportion and Scale: Delving into the significance of proportion and scale, understanding how these principles dictate the visual weight and size relationships within a design.

3.3. Unity and Variety: Navigating the delicate dance between unity and variety, exploring how designers create cohesion while introducing elements of surprise and interest.

IV. Innovative Design Techniques: Beyond Tradition

4.1. Asymmetry and Irregular Shapes: Analyzing the impact of asymmetry and irregular shapes in modern shoe design, breaking away from traditional norms for a contemporary aesthetic.

4.2. Material Innovation: Unraveling the world of innovative materials, from sustainable options to advanced textiles, and how these choices push the boundaries of creativity.

4.3. Technological Integration: Delving into the fusion of technology and design, exploring how 3D printing, smart textiles, and other innovations redefine the possibilities in shoemaking.

V. Design Process: From Concept to Creation

5.1. Research and Inspiration: Investigating the initial steps in the design process, from gathering inspiration to conducting market research and understanding consumer needs.

5.2. Sketching and Prototyping: Navigating the sketching and prototyping stages, where ideas take shape on paper and evolve into tangible forms through iterative processes.

5.3. Collaboration and Feedback: Unveiling the importance of collaboration and feedback in the design journey, fostering a dynamic exchange of ideas for continuous improvement.

VI. Trend Forecasting and Adaptation: Staying Ahead

6.1. Trend Analysis in Footwear: Analyzing the role of trend forecasting, exploring how designers stay ahead of the curve to create relevant and marketable designs.

6.2. Adaptation and Evolution: Delving into the art of adaptation, understanding how designers evolve their style while maintaining a brand's identity in response to changing trends.

AS WE EMBARK ON THIS exploration of design principles in shoemaking, we invite both enthusiasts and industry professionals to delve into the intricacies of the creative process. "Design Principles" is not just a guide; it is a celebration of the artistry that transforms ideas into tangible expressions of style, comfort, and innovation in the world of footwear.

Balancing Aesthetics and Functionality

BALANCING AESTHETICS and Functionality: The Art and Science of Exceptional Footwear Design

In the intricate world of footwear design, the delicate dance between aesthetics and functionality is a symphony that defines the essence of exceptional shoes. Each curve, line, and material choice contributes to not only the visual appeal but also the wearer's experience. "Balancing Aesthetics and Functionality" is an exploration into the principles, decisions, and craftsmanship that create footwear transcending mere utility, becoming wearable art that seamlessly integrates style with purpose.

CONTENTS:

3.2. Construction Techniques: Navigating the impact of construction methods on functionality, analyzing how choices like welted or stitched construction influence both form and wear.

3.3. Technological Integration: Delving into how technology enhances functionality, from shock-absorbing soles to moisture-wicking materials, revolutionizing the practical aspects of footwear.

IV. Design Principles that Harmonize

4.1. Balance and Symmetry: Analyzing the importance of balance and symmetry, exploring how these principles create visual harmony and stability in shoe design.

4.2. Proportion and Scale: Delving into the significance of proportion and scale, understanding how they dictate the visual weight and size relationships within a design.

4.3. Unity and Variety: Navigating the delicate balance between unity and variety, exploring how designers create cohesion while introducing elements of surprise and interest.

V. Beyond the Norm: Pushing the Boundaries

5.1. Innovative Shapes and Structures: Analyzing the impact of unconventional shapes and structures on both aesthetics and functionality, breaking away from traditional norms.

5.2. Artistic Embellishments: Delving into artistic embellishments, from handcrafted details to avant-garde elements, exploring how they elevate the design while maintaining practicality.

5.3. Cultural and Historical Influences: Unveiling how cultural and historical references enrich design, creating shoes that not only reflect current trends but also pay homage to heritage.

VI. Crafting for the Consumer: User-Centric Design

6.1. Understanding User Needs: Investigating the importance of understanding consumer needs, from ergonomic considerations to style preferences.

6.2. Customization and Personalization: Navigating the trend of customization and personalization, exploring how brands cater to individual tastes without compromising functionality.

6.3. Feedback Loops and Iterative Design: Delving into the iterative design process, where feedback loops from wearers contribute to continuous improvement in both aesthetics and functionality.

AS WE EMBARK ON THIS journey of understanding the delicate equilibrium between aesthetics and functionality in footwear design, "Balancing Aesthetics and Functionality" invites readers to appreciate the meticulous decisions and craftsmanship that transform shoes into more than just accessories—they become an extension of personal style and a testament to the seamless integration of beauty and purpose.

Chapter 4

Mastering Patterns and Templates

Creating Basic Patterns

Creating Basic Patterns: The Foundation of Exceptional Shoemaking
In the intricate world of shoemaking, the artistry begins with the creation of patterns—a meticulous process that forms the blueprint for every pair of shoes. "Creating Basic Patterns" serves as a comprehensive guide, offering insights into the fundamental principles, techniques, and considerations that go into crafting these foundational templates. From understanding foot anatomy to translating design concepts into tangible forms, this exploration is an invitation into the heart of shoemaking craftsmanship.

CONTENTS:

III. Tools of the Trade: Equipping the Pattern Maker

3.1. Measuring Tools: Investigating the various measuring tools, from calipers to rulers, essential for precise measurements and translating them into patterns.

3.2. Pattern Making Materials: Navigating the array of materials used in pattern making, including paper, cardboard, and modern alternatives, each chosen for its specific characteristics.

3.3. Digital Tools in Pattern Making: Delving into the integration of technology, exploring how digital tools enhance efficiency and accuracy in modern pattern making.

IV. Basic Pattern Components: Building Blocks of Design

4.1. Upper Patterns: Analyzing the creation of upper patterns, encompassing the vamp, quarters, and various components that shape the visual and functional aspects of the shoe.

4.2. Sole Patterns: Investigating the design and construction of sole patterns, exploring different types of soles and their impact on the overall structure and durability.

4.3. Heel Patterns: Navigating the intricacies of designing heel patterns, from flat to high heels, and how they contribute to both aesthetics and comfort.

V. Pattern Drafting Techniques: Translating Designs into Reality

5.1. Flat Pattern Drafting: Analyzing the traditional technique of flat pattern drafting, exploring how it translates two-dimensional designs into three-dimensional forms.

5.2. Last-Based Pattern Making: Delving into last-based pattern making, where the last—a mold of the foot—serves as a foundation for creating patterns with a precise fit.

5.3. Adapting Patterns for Design Variations: Investigating the flexibility of patterns, exploring how they can be adapted to create variations in design, including different closures and embellishments.

VI. Fitting and Adjustments: Refining Patterns for Comfort

6.1. Mock-Up Prototypes: Unveiling the importance of mock-up prototypes, exploring how they allow pattern makers to test and refine the fit before finalizing the patterns.

6.2. Pattern Adjustments: Navigating the iterative process of adjusting patterns based on fitting trials, ensuring an optimal balance between style and comfort.

6.3. Feedback Loops with Wear Testers: Delving into the collaborative process of seeking feedback from wear testers, refining patterns based on real-world comfort and performance.

AS WE EMBARK ON THIS journey of understanding the intricacies of pattern making, "Creating Basic Patterns" becomes a companion for both aspiring shoemakers and seasoned craftsmen. This guide not only demystifies the art of transforming designs into tangible patterns but also emphasizes the importance of precision, adaptability, and a deep understanding of foot anatomy in the pursuit of crafting footwear that seamlessly marries form and function.

Patterns for Different Shoe Types

PATTERNS FOR DIFFERENT Shoe Types: Crafting Precision for Every Style

In the realm of shoemaking, the artistry extends beyond the mastery of basic patterns to the nuanced understanding of diverse shoe types. "Patterns for Different Shoe Types" delves into the intricacies of creating templates for various styles, from timeless classics to contemporary designs. This comprehensive guide navigates the distinctive patterns required for heels, flats, boots, and athletic footwear, unveiling the secrets behind crafting precision for each unique shoe type.

CONTENTS:

3.2. Moccasin Patterns: Delving into the craftsmanship of moccasin patterns, where the construction method and choice of materials define the laid-back yet stylish appeal.

3.3. Espadrille Patterns: Investigating the intricacies of espadrille patterns, from the characteristic jute sole to the canvas upper, capturing the essence of casual chic.

IV. Crafting Patterns for Boots: From Ankle to Knee-High

4.1. Ankle Boot Patterns: Analyzing the design considerations for ankle boots, including variations in heel height, closures, and toe shapes that influence style and functionality.

4.2. Knee-High Boot Patterns: Delving into the challenges of crafting knee-high boot patterns, exploring how proportions and materials contribute to a flattering fit.

4.3. Western Boot Patterns: Investigating the distinctive elements of western boot patterns, from pointed toes to intricate stitching patterns that evoke a sense of rugged charm.

V. Athletic Footwear Patterns: Merging Style and Performance

5.1. Running Shoe Patterns: Navigating the specialized patterns for running shoes, exploring innovations in sole design, cushioning, and support for optimal performance.

5.2. Basketball Shoe Patterns: Delving into the unique requirements of basketball shoe patterns, where ankle support, traction, and durability play pivotal roles.

5.3. Sneaker Patterns: Investigating the versatile world of sneaker patterns, from classic designs to contemporary trends, capturing the essence of athleisure style.

VI. Customizing Patterns for Unique Designs: Beyond Conventions

6.1. Pattern Adaptation for Designer Shoes: Analyzing the flexibility of patterns for custom and designer shoes, exploring how shoemakers adapt templates to realize unique visions.

6.2. Incorporating Embellishments: Delving into the art of incorporating embellishments into patterns, from intricate stitching to beading, elevating shoes from functional to wearable art.

6.3. Sustainability in Pattern Making: Investigating the role of sustainable practices in pattern making, exploring eco-friendly materials and construction methods.

AS WE EMBARK ON THIS exploration of patterns for diverse shoe types, this guide becomes an indispensable companion for both aspiring and seasoned shoemakers. "Patterns for Different Shoe Types" not only provides technical insights but also celebrates the creativity and precision required to bring forth a tapestry of styles, each uniquely defined by its distinctive patterns. and function.

Scaling Patterns for Custom Sizing

SCALING PATTERNS FOR Custom Sizing: Precision in Every Stitch

In the realm of shoemaking, one size does not fit all. The art of crafting footwear extends beyond design and pattern creation; it embraces the intricacies of scaling patterns for custom sizing. "Scaling Patterns for Custom Sizing" is an exploration into the meticulous process of adapting templates to diverse foot dimensions, ensuring that every pair of shoes embodies both style and the perfect fit. This guide navigates the complexities of scaling patterns, revealing the techniques and considerations that transform a design into a bespoke creation tailored to individual measurements.

CONTENTS:

3.2. Manual Scaling Techniques: Navigating traditional manual scaling techniques, exploring how experienced craftsmen use measurements to adjust patterns with precision.

3.3. Considering Design Elements: Delving into the challenge of maintaining design integrity while scaling patterns, ensuring that style elements remain consistent across different sizes.

IV. Scaling Patterns for Various Shoe Types: Adapting to Diversity

4.1. Heels and Pumps: Analyzing the considerations for scaling patterns for heels and pumps, from adjusting pitch angles to ensuring stability in different heel heights.

4.2. Flats and Loafers: Delving into the challenges and solutions in scaling patterns for flats and loafers, where maintaining proportions is crucial for both style and fit.

4.3. Boots for Every Calf Size: Investigating the techniques for scaling patterns for boots, accounting for variations in calf size and ensuring a comfortable fit for various leg shapes.

V. Scaling Athletic Footwear Patterns: Beyond Aesthetics

5.1. Running Shoes for Different Gait Types: Navigating the complexities of scaling patterns for running shoes, considering variations in gait and pronation for optimal performance and comfort.

5.2. Basketball Shoes and Ankle Support: Delving into the specific challenges of scaling patterns for basketball shoes, emphasizing the importance of ankle support and stability.

5.3. Sneakers for Active Lifestyles: Investigating the customization of sneaker patterns for active lifestyles, balancing style with the functionality required for diverse activities.

VI. Fitting Sessions and Iterative Adjustments: Perfecting the Fit

6.1. Mock-Up Prototypes for Every Size: Analyzing the use of mock-up prototypes in fitting sessions, ensuring that each size iteration is tested for comfort and aesthetics.

6.2. Feedback Loops with Wear Testers: Navigating the collaborative process of seeking feedback from wear testers of various sizes, refining patterns based on real-world use.

6.3. Continuous Improvement: Delving into the philosophy of continuous improvement in custom sizing, where each fitting session informs refinements in both pattern scaling and design.

AS WE EMBARK ON THE journey of scaling patterns for custom sizing, this guide becomes an invaluable resource for shoemakers dedicated to crafting footwear that transcends standard sizes. "Scaling Patterns for Custom Sizing" not only demystifies the intricacies of adapting templates to diverse foot dimensions but also celebrates the artistry and precision required to deliver shoes that perfectly marry individual measurements with impeccable style.

Adjusting Patterns for Individual Feet

ADJUSTING PATTERNS for Individual Feet: The Art and Science of Customized Comfort

In the intricate world of shoemaking, the pursuit of comfort meets the precision of design when it comes to adjusting patterns for individual feet. "Adjusting Patterns for Individual Feet" unveils the meticulous process of tailoring shoe patterns to the unique contours and characteristics of each wearer's feet. This guide serves as a compass through the challenges and nuances of customization, ensuring that every pair of shoes not only looks stunning but also provides a personalized fit that transcends standard sizing.

CONTENTS:

3.2. Digital Tools in Pattern Adjustments: Navigating the integration of digital tools, such as 3D scanning and CAD software, in achieving precise and consistent adjustments.

3.3. Handcrafted Adjustments: Delving into traditional handcrafted techniques for pattern adjustments, showcasing the expertise required for manual modifications.

IV. Adjusting Patterns for Common Shoe Types: From Heels to Flats

4.1. Heel Adjustments for Stability: Analyzing the considerations for adjusting patterns in heels, addressing challenges like pitch, width, and height variations.

4.2. Flats and Loafers for a Snug Fit: Delving into the nuances of adjusting patterns for flats and loafers, ensuring optimal fit without compromising on style.

4.3. Boots Catering to Individual Calf Sizes: Investigating the techniques for adjusting patterns in boots, accommodating variations in calf sizes and delivering a tailored fit.

V. Customizing Athletic Footwear Patterns: Balancing Performance and Fit

5.1. Running Shoes Aligned with Gait: Navigating the complexities of adjusting patterns for running shoes, aligning the design with individual gait patterns for enhanced performance.

5.2. Basketball Shoes and Ankle Support: Delving into the specific challenges of adjusting patterns for basketball shoes, emphasizing the crucial role of ankle support.

5.3. Sneakers for Active Lifestyles: Investigating the customization of sneaker patterns, balancing style with the functionality required for various activities.

VI. Iterative Fitting Sessions: Perfecting the Personalized Fit

6.1. Prototyping and Wear Testing: Analyzing the use of prototypes in fitting sessions, utilizing wearer feedback to make iterative adjustments for the best possible fit.

6.2. Addressing Feedback Loops: Navigating the collaborative process of seeking feedback from wear testers, refining patterns based on real-world use.

6.3. Continuous Improvement Philosophy: Delving into the philosophy of continuous improvement in pattern adjustments, ensuring that each iteration brings shoes closer to the ideal personalized fit.

As we embark on this journey of adjusting patterns for individual feet, this guide becomes an essential companion for shoemakers committed to crafting footwear that transcends the boundaries of standard sizing. "Adjusting Patterns for Individual Feet" not only demystifies the intricacies of customization but also celebrates the union of art and science in creating shoes that are not just worn but truly experienced.

Chapter 5

The Craft of Cutting and Stitching

Precision Cutting Techniques

Precision Cutting Techniques: Crafting Perfection with Every Slice
In the realm of shoemaking, precision cutting stands as the cornerstone of creating footwear that seamlessly merges style, comfort, and durability. "Precision Cutting Techniques" unveils the artistry and methodology behind the meticulous cuts that transform raw materials into masterpieces. From selecting the right tools to mastering intricate patterns, this guide serves as an invaluable resource for shoemakers seeking to elevate their craft through precision cutting.

CONTENTS:

2.2. Cutting Mats and Surfaces: Delving into the importance of cutting surfaces, exploring how the right mat can prolong the life of blades and ensure accuracy.

2.3. Scissors and Shears: Investigating the role of scissors and shears in shoemaking, focusing on their applications in cutting different materials.

III. Types of Leather Cuts: From Straight to Intricate Patterns

3.1. Straight Cuts for Clean Lines: Analyzing the techniques behind straight cuts, emphasizing their importance in achieving clean lines and well-defined shapes.

3.2. Curved Cuts and Contours: Delving into the challenges and mastery involved in curved cuts, vital for crafting shoes that conform to the natural contours of the foot.

3.3. Intricate Patterns and Detailing: Investigating the precision required for intricate patterns and detailing, from delicate designs to functional elements.

IV. Mastering Cutting Techniques: A Step-by-Step Guide

4.1. Measuring and Marking: Navigating the importance of accurate measurements and markings as the foundation for precise cutting.

4.2. Straight Knife Techniques: Analyzing the various straight knife techniques, from long, smooth strokes to short, controlled movements for intricate sections.

4.3. Rotary Cutter Proficiency: Delving into the proficiency needed for using rotary cutters, ensuring efficiency and accuracy in various cutting scenarios.

V. Pattern Matching and Grain Alignment: Ensuring Cohesive Designs

5.1. Pattern Matching Strategies: Investigating the strategies for pattern matching, emphasizing how aligned patterns contribute to a cohesive and visually appealing design.

5.2. Understanding Grain Direction: Delving into the significance of grain direction, exploring how it affects the look, feel, and longevity of the finished product.

5.3. Mitigating Stretch and Distortion: Navigating techniques to mitigate stretch and distortion during cutting, ensuring consistency in the final shoe construction.

VI. Troubleshooting Cutting Challenges: Overcoming Hurdles with Finesse

6.1. Dealing with Different Leather Types: Analyzing how cutting techniques vary with different leather types, addressing challenges posed by varying thickness and textures.

6.2. Preventing Fraying and Uneven Edges: Delving into preventative measures against fraying and uneven edges, maintaining the integrity of cut pieces.

6.3. Reviving Dull Blades: Investigating techniques for blade maintenance and revival, ensuring sharp and precise cuts throughout the shoemaking process.

AS WE EMBARK ON THE journey of precision cutting, this guide becomes a trusted companion for shoemakers, guiding them through the nuances of the craft. "Precision Cutting Techniques" not only demystifies the art of cutting but also empowers artisans to transform raw materials into exquisite footwear, one precise cut at a time.

Tips for Accurate Cutting

MASTERING THE ART: Tips for Accurate Cutting in Shoemaking

In the meticulous craft of shoemaking, the precision of cutting is akin to sculpting raw materials into wearable masterpieces. "Tips for Accurate Cutting" delves into the nuances of this essential skill, providing seasoned advice and insights to elevate your cutting techniques. From choosing the right tools to mastering the art of pattern alignment, this guide is a compass for artisans striving for excellence in the intricate dance of blades and leather.

CONTENTS:

I. Introduction: The Crucial Role of Accuracy in Shoemaking

1.1. The Foundation of Craftsmanship: Understanding how accuracy in cutting forms the foundation of creating footwear that seamlessly combines form and function.

1.2. Balancing Act of Precision: Navigating the delicate balance between speed and accuracy, where every cut contributes to the overall quality of the finished product.

II. Selecting the Right Cutting Tools: A Shoemaker's Arsenal

2.1. Quality Over Quantity: Emphasizing the importance of investing in high-quality cutting tools, ensuring durability and precision in every slice.

2.2. The Versatility of Rotary Cutters: Delving into the advantages of rotary cutters, exploring how their versatility aids in various cutting scenarios.

2.3. Scissors and Shears Mastery: Investigating the nuances of using scissors and shears, showcasing their role in achieving accuracy in different aspects of shoemaking.

III. Preparing Materials for Cutting: Setting the Stage for Accuracy

3.1. Understanding Leather Grain: Analyzing the impact of leather grain on cutting accuracy, emphasizing the need to align cutting direction with the grain.

3.2. Proper Marking Techniques: Delving into the importance of accurate marking, exploring techniques to ensure that each cut is guided by precise measurements.

3.3. Consistency in Cutting Surfaces: Investigating the role of cutting surfaces, from self-healing mats to specialized tables, in maintaining consistency and accuracy.

IV. Essential Techniques for Accurate Cuts: Mastering the Basics

4.1. Straight Cuts for Clean Lines: Analyzing the techniques behind straight cuts, focusing on achieving clean lines and well-defined shapes.

4.2. Curved Cuts and Contours: Delving into the challenges and mastery involved in curved cuts, vital for crafting shoes that conform to the natural contours of the foot.

4.3. Pattern Matching Brilliance: Investigating the precision required for pattern matching, ensuring that aligned patterns contribute to a cohesive and visually appealing design.

V. Achieving Consistency in Batch Cutting: Scaling Accuracy

5.1. Batch Cutting Efficiency: Navigating the strategies for achieving consistency when cutting multiple pieces, emphasizing the importance of a systematic approach.

5.2. Customizing Cutting Techniques for Designs: Analyzing how different designs may require adjustments in cutting techniques, ensuring accuracy while adapting to varied patterns.

5.3. Minimizing Material Waste: Investigating methods to minimize material waste during cutting, promoting sustainability without compromising on precision.

VI. Troubleshooting Accuracy Challenges: Overcoming Cutting Hurdles

6.1. Dealing with Different Materials: Analyzing how cutting techniques may vary with different materials, addressing challenges posed by varying thickness and textures.

6.2. Addressing Blade Dullness: Delving into the importance of blade maintenance, providing tips for addressing dullness and ensuring consistently accurate cuts.

6.3. Preventing Fraying and Distortion: Investigating preventative measures against fraying and distortion, maintaining the integrity of cut pieces from start to finish.

EMBARK ON A JOURNEY of refinement and precision with "Tips for Accurate Cutting." This guide is not merely a collection of techniques but a roadmap for shoemakers eager to transform every cut into an expression of craftsmanship. May your blades be sharp, your measurements precise, and your cuts the foundation of footwear that stands as a testament to the artistry of shoemaking.

Stitching Methods

MASTERING THE ART OF Shoemaking: Unraveling the Tapestry of Stitching Methods

In the intricate world of shoemaking, where every stitch weaves a story of precision and durability, the choice of stitching method is a critical element that defines the very essence of a well-crafted shoe. "Stitching Methods" is a comprehensive exploration into the diverse techniques that elevate the humble thread into a vital component of footwear excellence. From traditional hand-stitching to cutting-edge machine methods, this guide is a roadmap for artisans seeking mastery in the art of stitching.

CONTENTS:

I. Introduction: The Thread that Binds Craftsmanship

1.1. The Unseen Architect: Understanding the pivotal role stitching plays in the structural integrity and longevity of a pair of shoes.

1.2. Evolution of Stitching in Shoemaking: Tracing the historical progression of stitching methods, from ancient handcrafting traditions to modern industrial techniques.

II. Hand Stitching Techniques: A Symphony of Precision

2.1. Saddle Stitch Mastery: Delving into the art of saddle stitching, a time-honored method known for its strength, durability, and aesthetically pleasing results.

2.2. Lock Stitch Elegance: Exploring the nuances of lock stitching, a technique that combines strength with a clean and refined finish, ideal for various shoe styles.

2.3. Blind Stitch Wizardry: Unraveling the secrets behind blind stitching, a technique that conceals stitches for a seamless and polished appearance.

III. Machine Stitching Innovations: Bridging Tradition and Technology

3.1. Lockstitch Machines Unveiled: Analyzing the role of lockstitch machines in modern shoemaking, offering efficiency without compromising on quality.

3.2. Goodyear Welt Construction: Delving into the iconic Goodyear welt, a machine-stitching method celebrated for its durability, water resistance, and ease of resoling.

3.3. Blake Stitching Revolution: Investigating the Blake stitch, a machine method known for its flexibility and suitability for sleek, lightweight designs.

IV. Specialty Stitching for Unique Designs: Elevating Artistry

4.1. Decorative Stitching Flourishes: Exploring the world of decorative stitches, adding a touch of artistry to footwear designs with unique patterns and motifs.

4.2. Handcrafted Embellishments: Unveiling hand-stitched embellishments, from intricate broguing to detailed patterns, showcasing the artful side of stitching.

4.3. Custom Stitching for Personalization: Investigating the possibilities of custom stitching, allowing shoemakers to create unique designs tailored to individual preferences.

V. Troubleshooting Stitching Challenges: Overcoming Common Hurdles

5.1. Addressing Tension Issues: Analyzing tension-related challenges in stitching, providing tips and techniques to achieve consistent and balanced stitches.

5.2. Dealing with Thread Breakage: Delving into the causes of thread breakage during stitching and offering solutions to maintain a smooth workflow.

5.3. Ensuring Stitch Alignment: Investigating methods to ensure precise stitch alignment, contributing to the overall aesthetics and functionality of the finished shoe.

VI. Future Trends in Shoemaking Stitching Methods: Innovations on the Horizon

6.1. Advancements in Machine Technology: Exploring emerging technologies that promise to revolutionize machine stitching, offering increased efficiency and precision.

6.2. Sustainability in Stitching: Investigating eco-friendly stitching practices and materials, aligning with the growing demand for sustainable and ethical shoemaking.

6.3. Digital Stitching Designs: Delving into the integration of digital technologies in stitching, opening new possibilities for intricate and customizable designs.

EMBARK ON A JOURNEY through the stitches that define excellence in shoemaking. "Stitching Methods" is not just a guide; it's a celebration of the craftsmanship that turns threads into the unseen heroes of footwear, ensuring every step is taken in comfort, style, and enduring quality. May your stitches be as impeccable as the stories they tell in the rich tapestry of shoemaking.

Hand Stitching vs. Machine Stitching

MASTERING THE CRAFT: Hand Stitching vs. Machine Stitching in Shoemaking

In the realm of shoemaking, the choice between hand stitching and machine stitching is a defining factor that shapes not only the final product but also the artisan's approach to their craft. "Hand Stitching vs. Machine Stitching" is an exploration into the intricacies of these two methods, dissecting their strengths, weaknesses, and the artistic nuances that make each a distinctive aspect of the shoemaker's toolkit.

I. INTRODUCTION: A Stitch in Time

The introduction sets the stage by highlighting the fundamental role stitching plays in the construction of shoes, paving the way for a deeper understanding of the age-old debate between hand stitching and machine stitching.

1.1. The Art of Stitching: An overview of the significance of stitching in shoemaking, emphasizing its impact on durability, aesthetics, and overall craftsmanship.

1.2. The Duality of Techniques: A brief introduction to the dichotomy between hand stitching and machine stitching, setting the tone for an in-depth exploration.

II. Hand Stitching: Crafting with Precision

Delving into the traditional method of hand stitching, this section celebrates the artistry and precision that define this time-honored technique.

2.1. Saddle Stitch Mastery: Unraveling the secrets behind saddle stitching, exploring its advantages in creating durable and aesthetically pleasing seams.

2.2. Lock Stitch Elegance: Examining the nuances of lock stitching by hand, showcasing its ability to combine strength with refined finishes.

2.3. Blind Stitch Wizardry: An exploration of blind stitching, a technique that conceals stitches for a seamless appearance, exemplifying the finesse of handcrafted shoes.

III. Machine Stitching: Bridging Efficiency and Consistency

This section dives into the realm of machine stitching, where efficiency and consistency become paramount without compromising on quality.

3.1. Lockstitch Machines Unveiled: Analyzing the role of lockstitch machines in modern shoemaking, offering insights into their efficiency and reliability.

3.2. Goodyear Welt Construction: Exploring the iconic Goodyear welt, a machine-stitching method celebrated for durability, water resistance, and ease of resoling.

3.3. Blake Stitching Revolution: Investigating the Blake stitch, a machine method known for flexibility and suitability for sleek, lightweight designs.

IV. Comparative Analysis: Strengths and Weaknesses

This section provides an unbiased examination of the strengths and weaknesses inherent in both hand stitching and machine stitching, guiding artisans in making informed choices.

4.1. Durability and Longevity: Comparing the longevity of hand-stitched and machine-stitched shoes, considering factors like thread tension and stitch density.

4.2. Artistry and Aesthetics: Evaluating the aesthetic outcomes of hand stitching and machine stitching, acknowledging the unique beauty each method imparts to the finished product.

4.3. Efficiency and Production: Weighing the efficiency of hand stitching against the mass production capabilities of machines, recognizing the demands of the market.

V. Crafting the Future: Innovations and Trends

This section peeks into the future of stitching in shoemaking, exploring emerging technologies and trends that might shape the industry.

5.1. Integration of Technology: Examining how technology is influencing both hand stitching and machine stitching, from advanced tools for artisans to automated stitching processes.

5.2. Sustainability in Stitching: Investigating the growing demand for sustainable stitching practices, from eco-friendly materials to energy-efficient machinery.

5.3. Artisanal Resurgence: Discussing the resurgence of appreciation for handcrafted shoes and its impact on the market, as consumers seek unique, personalized products.

VI. Conclusion: Crafting the Perfect Pair

The conclusion summarizes the key insights, emphasizing that the choice between hand stitching and machine stitching is not a matter of superiority but a matter of harmony with the artisan's vision and the demands of the market.

EMBARK ON A JOURNEY through the stitches that define excellence in shoemaking. "Hand Stitching vs. Machine Stitching" is a comprehensive guide that celebrates the diverse approaches to a timeless craft. May your stitches tell a story of precision, artistry, and a commitment to mastering the craft of shoemaking.

Chapter 6

Lasting and Assembling

Understanding Lasts

Mastering the Foundation: A Deep Dive into Understanding Lasts in Shoemaking

Shoemaking is an intricate dance of artistry and functionality, where every step contributes to the creation of a pair that not only adorns but also embraces the foot with comfort. At the heart of this process lies a crucial element often overlooked by the untrained eye – the last. "Understanding Lasts" is your comprehensive guide to unraveling the mysteries of these unsung heroes in the world of footwear craftsmanship.

I. INTRODUCTION: THE Silent Architects

The introduction sets the stage for the profound role lasts play in the art of shoemaking, introducing them as the silent architects shaping the very foundation of a pair of shoes.

1.1. Anatomy of a Last: An exploration of the components and anatomy of lasts, laying the groundwork for a deeper understanding.

1.2. The Lasting Impression: Discussing the lasting impact of a well-chosen last on the fit, style, and overall quality of the finished shoe.

II. History and Evolution of Lasts: From Tradition to Innovation

This section delves into the historical evolution of lasts, tracing their journey from traditional methods to modern innovations.

2.1. Traditional Last-Making Techniques: Exploring the traditional craftsmanship behind hand-carved lasts and their cultural significance.

2.2. Modern Materials and Techniques: Investigating how technology has revolutionized last-making, introducing materials like plastic and computer-aided design (CAD).

2.3. Lasts Across Cultures: Recognizing the diverse approaches to last-making worldwide, from bespoke European traditions to mass production in global markets.

III. Types of Lasts: Navigating the Diversity

This section categorizes and elucidates the various types of lasts, each designed for specific purposes and styles.

3.1. Straight Lasts for Simplicity: Explaining the characteristics and applications of straight lasts, ideal for simple and classic designs.

3.2. Curved Lasts for Elegance: Unveiling the benefits and uses of curved lasts, known for creating elegant and stylish footwear.

3.3. Anatomical Lasts for Comfort: Delving into the intricacies of anatomical lasts, engineered for superior comfort and foot support.

IV. Last Sizing and Fitting: Crafting the Perfect Match

This section guides shoemakers and wearers alike in understanding the nuances of last sizing and how it influences the fit of the final product.

4.1. Last Sizing Demystified: Clarifying the sizing conventions of lasts and their correlation with shoe sizes.

4.2. The Fit Equation: Exploring how last dimensions impact the fit of shoes, emphasizing the importance of a harmonious fit.

4.3. Custom Lasts for Individuality: Discussing the rising trend of custom lasts, offering a personalized fit for discerning customers.

V. Last Maintenance and Storage: Preserving Craftsmanship

Shoemakers need to comprehend the significance of last maintenance and proper storage to ensure the longevity of these essential tools.

5.1. Preserving the Craft: Offering practical tips on maintaining wooden lasts, including cleaning, conditioning, and storing them properly.

5.2. Modern Materials, Modern Care: Providing guidance on caring for lasts made from modern materials, ensuring durability and functionality.

5.3. Sustainability in Last Making: Discussing eco-friendly practices in last making, aligning with the growing demand for sustainable craftsmanship.

VI. Innovations in Last Technology: Shaping the Future

This section explores how technological advancements are reshaping the landscape of last-making, introducing innovations that propel the craft forward.

6.1. 3D Printing in Last Production: Examining how 3D printing technology is revolutionizing last production, offering unprecedented precision and customization.

6.2. Digital Design and Virtual Prototyping: Exploring the role of digital design and virtual prototyping in the creation of lasts, enhancing efficiency and creativity.

6.3. Smart Lasts for Smart Shoes: Discussing the integration of smart technologies into lasts, catering to the demands of the ever-evolving footwear market.

VII. Conclusion: The Foundation of Craftsmanship

The conclusion reinforces the vital role of lasts in the art of shoemaking, emphasizing their silent but indispensable contribution to the creation of every pair of shoes.

EMBARK ON A JOURNEY of discovery as we unravel the intricate world of lasts in shoemaking. "Understanding Lasts" is not just a guide; it's an ode to the silent architects shaping the very essence of footwear craftsmanship. May your understanding of lasts elevate your appreciation for the artistry and precision that go into each meticulously crafted pair of shoes.

Choosing the Right Last for Your Design

CRAFTING THE PERFECT Fit: A Comprehensive Guide to Choosing the Right Last for Your Shoe Designs

In the realm of shoemaking, the last is not merely a silent protagonist; it is the unsung hero that breathes life into the designs. "Choosing the Right Last for Your Design" serves as your compass in navigating the intricate world of lasts, ensuring that every step in crafting your shoes is a stride toward perfection.

I. INTRODUCTION: THE Foundation of Design

The introduction sets the stage for the pivotal role of choosing the right last in the design process, emphasizing its impact on the aesthetics, functionality, and overall success of a pair of shoes.

1.1. The Marriage of Form and Function: Discussing how the right last harmonizes design aspirations with the practical requirements of footwear.

1.2. Understanding Design Language: Introducing the key design elements influenced by the choice of last, such as toe shape, heel height, and overall silhouette.

II. Types of Lasts and Design Styles: Decoding the Options

This section unravels the symbiotic relationship between different types of lasts and distinct design styles, offering insights into how each contributes to the overall look and feel of the final product.

2.1. Lasts for Classic Elegance: Exploring the compatibility of straight lasts with timeless, classic designs, perfect for formal and traditional footwear.

2.2. Curved Lasts for Contemporary Flair: Delving into how curved lasts infuse a sense of modernity and flair, enhancing the visual appeal of contemporary designs.

2.3. Anatomical Lasts for Enhanced Comfort and Style: Detailing the advantages of using anatomical lasts to marry comfort and style, especially in athletic and casual footwear.

III. Matching Lasts to Design Elements: A Symphony of Components

This section dissects the anatomy of shoe designs, demonstrating how specific last features complement various design elements.

3.1. Toe Shapes and Last Selection: Connecting the dots between toe shapes (round, square, pointed) and the choice of last, ensuring a seamless integration for cohesive designs.

3.2. Heel Heights and Last Compatibility: Analyzing the impact of heel heights on overall design aesthetics, guiding designers in selecting the appropriate last for diverse heel styles.

3.3. Upper Design Considerations: Exploring how upper design elements, such as straps, laces, and patterns, interact with the last, influencing the overall visual appeal.

IV. Tailoring Lasts for Specific Shoe Types: A Designer's Arsenal

This section acts as a designer's arsenal, providing a toolbox of insights on tailoring lasts for specific shoe types, from boots to sandals.

4.1. Boot Lasts: Crafting Stability and Style: Unveiling the nuances of choosing lasts for boots, emphasizing stability, ankle support, and stylistic preferences.

4.2. Sandal Lasts: Embracing Openness and Comfort: Navigating the intricacies of selecting lasts for sandals, focusing on openness, breathability, and foot comfort.

4.3. Athletic Shoe Lasts: The Fusion of Performance and Design: Balancing the demands of athletic footwear with design considerations, ensuring the perfect marriage of performance and style.

V. Customizing Lasts for Unique Designs: Beyond Boundaries

This section empowers designers to break free from conventional molds, exploring the realm of custom last creation for truly unique and avant-garde designs.

5.1. Artistry in Custom Lasts: Showcasing examples of how designers have pushed boundaries by creating custom lasts, resulting in groundbreaking and innovative designs.

5.2. Collaboration with Lastmakers: Encouraging collaboration between designers and lastmakers to bring conceptual designs to life, highlighting real-world success stories.

VI. The Importance of Prototyping: Design Validation

Prototyping emerges as a crucial phase in the design process, allowing designers to validate their choices and make informed adjustments before mass production.

6.1. Prototyping Essentials: Outlining the steps involved in creating prototypes and testing the chosen last with different design elements.

6.2. Iterative Design Process: Embracing an iterative approach to design, emphasizing the significance of refining prototypes based on real-world testing and user feedback.

VII. Conclusion: Crafting a Design Legacy

The conclusion celebrates the symbiotic dance between design and last selection, encouraging designers to view each creation as a legacy shaped by thoughtful choices.

Embark on a journey where design aspirations meet the precision of last selection. "Choosing the Right Last for Your Design" is more than a guide; it is your companion in sculpting footwear that transcends trends, standing as a testament to the harmonious fusion of artistry and functionality. May your design journey be as rewarding as the steps you take in crafting the perfect fit.

Techniques for Lasting and Attaching Soles

MASTERING THE CRAFT: Techniques for Lasting and Attaching Soles

In the intricate dance of shoemaking, lasting and attaching soles represent the grand finale, where meticulous techniques intertwine with craftsmanship. This exploration unveils the secrets of this pivotal stage, a culmination of skill, precision, and artistry.

I. INTRODUCTION: THE Artistry of Lasting

The journey begins with a tribute to the artistry of lasting, setting the stage for an in-depth exploration of the techniques that breathe life into the shoes.

1.1. Lasting as a Finishing Touch: Understanding the transformative power of lasting in shaping the shoe's form and structure.

1.2. The Interplay of Design and Lasting: Unraveling the synergy between design intent and the lasting process, emphasizing the importance of harmony in every step.

II. Types of Lasting Techniques: A Symphony of Approaches

Dive into the myriad techniques that form the backbone of lasting, each contributing a unique note to the symphony of shoemaking.

2.1. Mckay Stitching: A Timeless Tradition: Exploring the enduring elegance of Mckay stitching, tracing its historical roots and its contemporary relevance.

2.2. Goodyear Welt: The Epitome of Craftsmanship: Unveiling the intricacies of Goodyear welt construction, celebrated for its durability, water-resistance, and ease of resoling.

2.3. Blake Stitch: The Italian Flair: Capturing the essence of Blake stitching, known for its sleek profile and flexibility, ideal for dress shoes and loafers.

III. Sole Attachment Methods: Where Form Meets Function

Transitioning seamlessly from lasting to sole attachment, this section dissects various methods, each serving a distinct purpose in the union of sole and upper.

3.1. Cementing Techniques: A Bond of Trust: Navigating the world of cementing, discussing its applications in both traditional and modern shoemaking.

3.2. Blake Rapid Construction: A Fusion of Speed and Quality: Delving into the nuanced process of Blake Rapid construction, offering a compromise between the sleekness of Blake stitching and the sturdiness of Goodyear welt.

3.3. Welted Sole Attachment: The Gold Standard: Illuminating the welted sole attachment method, considered the gold standard for its durability, repairability, and timeless aesthetic.

IV. The Art of Lasting: Precision and Patience

This section becomes a masterclass in the art of lasting, emphasizing the precision required and the patience essential for achieving perfection.

4.1. Tool Mastery: Navigating the Lasting Arsenal: Diving into the essential tools used in lasting, from pincers to lasting pliers, outlining their functions and the finesse required for their use.

4.2. Lasting Machines: Enhancing Efficiency: Exploring the role of lasting machines in modern shoemaking, highlighting their contributions to efficiency without compromising craftsmanship.

4.3. Hands-On Techniques: From Novice to Virtuoso: Providing step-by-step insights into manual lasting techniques, suitable for both aspiring shoemakers and seasoned craftsmen looking to refine their skills.

V. Troubleshooting: Navigating Challenges with Expertise

Like any craft, shoemaking is not without its challenges. This section equips readers with the expertise needed to troubleshoot common issues during the lasting and sole attachment phases.

5.1. Common Lasting Pitfalls: Identifying and addressing challenges such as creasing, misalignment, and tension issues during the lasting process.

5.2. Sole Attachment Woes: Offering solutions for challenges encountered during sole attachment, ensuring a smooth and flawless finish.

VI. The Symbiosis of Design and Technique: Case Studies

This section presents real-world case studies, showcasing how the marriage of design vision and technical expertise culminates in exceptional and iconic footwear.

6.1. Iconic Shoes Through the Lens of Lasting: Analyzing renowned shoe designs and their lasting techniques, demonstrating the profound impact of technique on the final product.

6.2. Innovative Sole Attachments: Pushing Boundaries: Highlighting instances where shoemakers have pushed the boundaries of traditional sole attachments, resulting in groundbreaking designs.

VII. The Future of Shoemaking: Innovations in Lasting and Sole Attachment

Concluding the journey with a glimpse into the future, this section explores emerging innovations in lasting and sole attachment, inviting readers to envision the evolution of shoemaking.

7.1. Sustainable Approaches to Lasting: Discussing eco-friendly materials and sustainable practices in lasting and sole attachment, addressing the growing demand for environmentally conscious shoemaking.

7.2. Technological Advancements: A New Frontier: Exploring how technology, from 3D printing to automation, is reshaping the landscape of lasting and sole attachment.

EMBARK ON A VOYAGE through the soul of shoemaking, where lasting and attaching soles transcend craftsmanship to become an art form. "Mastering the Craft: Techniques for Lasting and Attaching Soles" is more than a guide; it's an ode to the convergence of skill, precision, and passion that defines the world of shoemaking. May each page be a step forward in mastering the intricate dance between form and function.

Chapter 7

Finishing Touches

Sanding and Buffing

Perfecting the Finish: Sanding and Buffing Techniques in Shoemaking
In the realm of shoemaking, every meticulous step contributes to the creation of a masterpiece. Sanding and buffing, often considered the unsung heroes of the process, play a crucial role in refining and perfecting the final product. Join us on an exploration of these nuanced techniques that elevate shoes from crafted to exceptional.

I. INTRODUCTION: THE Crucial Role of Sanding and Buffing
Unveil the significance of sanding and buffing as the final acts of refinement in the shoemaking symphony, ensuring a flawless finish that captivates with every step.

1.1. Beyond Aesthetics: Functional Refinement: Understand how sanding contributes not only to the visual appeal but also enhances the functionality and comfort of the shoes.

1.2. The Harmony of Techniques: Explore the seamless transition from sanding to buffing, discovering how these techniques harmonize to achieve a refined and polished surface.

II. The Art of Sanding: Transforming Rough to Refined
Delve into the world of sanding, where raw materials undergo a metamorphosis, revealing the intricacies of achieving smoothness and uniformity.

2.1. Choosing the Right Sandpaper: Navigate the array of sandpaper options, from coarse to fine grits, and understand their applications in the different stages of sanding.

2.2. Sanding Techniques for Different Leathers: Uncover specialized sanding approaches tailored to various leather types, ensuring an optimal finish without compromising the material.

2.3. Addressing Imperfections: Learn how skilled artisans tackle imperfections through strategic sanding, creating a canvas ready for the final strokes of refinement.

III. Buffing: The Culmination of Craftsmanship

Witness the artistry of buffing, where the magic of sheen and luster takes center stage, transforming shoes into objects of desire.

3.1. Buffing Materials and Compounds: Explore the diverse range of materials and compounds employed in buffing, unlocking the secrets to achieving a brilliant shine.

3.2. Hand-Buffing vs. Machine Buffing: Compare the nuanced outcomes of hand-buffing and machine buffing, shedding light on the decision-making process behind each approach.

3.3. Achieving the Perfect Shine: Follow a step-by-step guide to achieving the elusive mirror-like shine that defines high-quality craftsmanship.

IV. The Symbiosis of Craft and Technology

This section explores how modern technology has seamlessly integrated with traditional craftsmanship, offering innovative solutions in sanding and buffing.

4.1. Automated Sanding Processes: Delve into the world of automated sanding processes, showcasing how technology enhances efficiency without compromising precision.

4.2. High-Tech Buffing Equipment: Explore cutting-edge buffing machines and equipment, revolutionizing the way artisans bring out the final gleam in their creations.

V. Troubleshooting: Navigating Challenges in Sanding and Buffing

Acknowledge the common challenges faced during sanding and buffing, accompanied by expert insights and solutions.

5.1. Preventing Over-Sanding: Understand the delicate balance between achieving smoothness and risking over-sanding, leading to potential issues like thinning of materials.

5.2. Dealing with Uneven Buffing Results: Tackle challenges related to uneven buffing, ensuring a consistent and professional finish across the entire shoe.

VI. Beyond Shoes: Sanding and Buffing in Leather Accessories

Expand the horizon to leather accessories, exploring how sanding and buffing techniques extend their influence to wallets, belts, and other handcrafted leather goods.

6.1. The Art of Accessory Finishing: Witness the transferability of sanding and buffing techniques, enriching the quality and allure of leather accessories.

VII. The Future of Finishing: Innovations and Sustainability

Concluding our journey, this section glimpses into the future, exploring emerging trends and sustainable practices in sanding and buffing.

7.1. Eco-Friendly Sanding Practices: Discuss sustainable approaches to sanding, considering the environmental impact and eco-friendly alternatives.

7.2. Green Buffing Compounds: Embrace the future with green buffing compounds, offering a glimpse into the eco-conscious direction of buffing practices.

EMBARK ON A QUEST THROUGH the delicate art of sanding and buffing, where precision and finesse culminate in a finish that transcends mere craftsmanship. "Perfecting the Finish: Sanding and Buffing Techniques in Shoemaking" is not just a guide; it's an ode to the meticulous hands and discerning eyes that ensure each pair of shoes is a testament to mastery. May this journey inspire and guide both aspiring artisans and seasoned craftsmen toward the pinnacle of shoemaking excellence.

Polishing and Coloring

ELEVATING CRAFTSMANSHIP: The Art of Polishing and Coloring in Shoemaking

In the realm of shoemaking, the journey from raw materials to refined footwear involves a symphony of techniques, with polishing and coloring being the crescendo. These crucial steps not only bestow aesthetic allure but also unveil the soul of each creation. Join us on a deep dive into the meticulous artistry of polishing and coloring, where every stroke, every pigment, adds character and sophistication to the canvas of leather.

I. INTRODUCTION: UNVEILING the Essence of Polishing and Coloring

Discover the transformative power of polishing and coloring as the final acts in the shoemaking tapestry, enriching shoes with character, depth, and individuality.

1.1. Beyond Aesthetics: A Story in Every Shine: Explore how the interplay of polish and color narrates a story, turning each pair of shoes into a unique expression of craftsmanship.

1.2. Preserving Leather Integrity: Delve into the delicate balance between enhancing aesthetics and preserving the inherent qualities of the leather.

II. Polishing: The Elegance of Reflective Surfaces

Understand the nuances of polishing, where skilled hands and quality products merge to create a mirror-like finish that captivates the beholder.

2.1. Choosing the Right Polish: Navigate the myriad of polishing products, deciphering the distinctions between wax, cream, and liquid polishes for different leather types.

2.2. Hand-Polishing Techniques: Uncover the artisanal techniques of hand-polishing, from circular motions to gentle buffing, ensuring a consistent and lustrous shine.

2.3. Machine Polishing for Efficiency: Explore the world of machine polishing, where advanced tools contribute to efficiency without compromising precision.

III. Coloring: Crafting Hues and Tones

Dive into the realm of coloring, where pigments breathe life into the leather, creating a palette that mirrors the designer's vision and style.

3.1. Types of Leather Dyes: Explore the variety of leather dyes, from penetrating dyes for a deep, even color to antique finishes that add vintage charm.

3.2. Techniques for Achieving Depth: Learn the techniques for layering colors, creating depth, and adding visual interest to the leather surface.

3.3. Customization with Patinas: Discover the art of patina application, allowing shoemakers to personalize each creation with unique and artistic finishes.

IV. Balancing Act: Harmony Between Polish and Color

Recognize the delicate interplay between polishing and coloring, where balance ensures a harmonious outcome that enhances both aesthetics and durability.

4.1. Polishing After Coloring: Understand the significance of post-coloring polishing, a step often underestimated but pivotal for refining the final appearance.

4.2. Preserving Color Intensity: Explore strategies to preserve the vibrancy of colors over time, offering insights into maintenance practices for long-lasting beauty.

V. Trends in Polishing and Coloring: Bridging Tradition and Modernity

Delve into evolving trends, where traditional techniques meet contemporary preferences, shaping the future of polishing and coloring in shoemaking.

5.1. Artisanal Revival: Witness the resurgence of artisanal approaches to polishing and coloring, reflecting a renewed appreciation for craftsmanship.

5.2. Innovations in Coloring Technology: Explore cutting-edge developments in coloring technologies, from sustainable dyes to advanced application methods.

VI. Troubleshooting: Navigating Challenges with Expertise

Address common challenges shoemakers encounter during polishing and coloring, providing practical solutions to ensure a flawless outcome.

6.1. Avoiding Uneven Color Distribution: Tackle issues related to uneven color distribution, offering insights into application techniques and product selection.

6.2. Dealing with Polish Residue: Navigate challenges posed by polish residue, guiding artisans on effective removal without compromising the shine.

VII. Beyond Shoes: Applications in Leather Goods

Extend the knowledge of polishing and coloring techniques to diverse leather goods, exploring their application in wallets, bags, and other accessories.

7.1. Customization in Leather Accessories: Witness how polishing and coloring techniques enhance the customization of leather accessories, adding a touch of luxury.

VIII. Sustainability in Polishing and Coloring: A Step Towards Eco-Friendly Practices

Conclude the journey by exploring sustainable practices in polishing and coloring, underscoring the importance of environmental consciousness in modern craftsmanship.

8.1. Eco-Friendly Polish Options: Examine eco-conscious polish alternatives, contributing to the reduction of environmental impact without compromising quality.

8.2. Vegetable-Based Dyes and Sustainable Practices: Embrace sustainability through the use of vegetable-based dyes and practices that minimize the ecological footprint.

EMBARK ON AN ODYSSEY through the realms of polish and color, where precision meets artistry, and each pair of shoes becomes a canvas for creative expression. "Elevating Craftsmanship: The Art of Polishing and Coloring in Shoemaking" is not just a guide; it's a celebration of the meticulous hands that impart life to leather, turning the ordinary into the extraordinary. May this exploration inspire aspiring artisans and seasoned craftsmen alike to embark on their own journeys of shoemaking mastery.

Enhancing the Aesthetic Appeal

ELEVATING EXCELLENCE: The Art of Enhancing Aesthetic Appeal in Shoemaking

In the realm of shoemaking, craftsmanship extends beyond functionality; it embraces an artful journey of enhancing the aesthetic appeal. Every stitch, every cut, and every choice of material contributes to the creation of footwear that transcends mere utility, evolving into wearable masterpieces. In this exploration, we delve into the intricate techniques and nuanced decisions that weave together to elevate the aesthetic allure of shoes, merging form and function seamlessly.

I. INTRODUCTION: THE Fusion of Form and Function

Embark on a journey that transcends the utilitarian purpose of shoes, unveiling the delicate balance between form and function.

1.1. Defining Aesthetic Appeal: Explore the multifaceted concept of aesthetic appeal, delving into the elements that contribute to visual allure in shoemaking.

1.2. Harmony with Functionality: Understand how enhancing aesthetics aligns with maintaining the structural integrity and comfort of footwear.

II. Material Selection: A Palette of Possibilities

Navigate the vast array of materials available to shoemakers, examining their impact on the visual aesthetics of the final product.

2.1. Leather Varieties and Finishes: Explore the diverse world of leather, from classic finishes to exotic varieties, and understand how each choice influences aesthetics.

2.2. Innovative Material Integration: Delve into the integration of innovative materials, from sustainable alternatives to high-tech fabrics, revolutionizing the visual landscape.

III. Design Principles: The Blueprint of Beauty

Uncover the principles that guide shoemakers in crafting designs that seamlessly merge aesthetics with wearability.

3.1. Proportion and Symmetry: Explore the fundamental principles of proportion and symmetry, ensuring that designs harmonize with the natural contours of the foot.

3.2. Embracing Trends without Compromise: Navigate the delicate balance of incorporating trends while maintaining timeless elegance in shoemaking design.

IV. Handcrafted Techniques: Artistry in Every Stitch

Discover the artistry embedded in handcrafted techniques, where skilled hands transform raw materials into bespoke footwear.

4.1. Artisanal Stitching Patterns: Unravel the beauty of artisanal stitching patterns, from classic techniques like the Goodyear welt to intricate decorative stitches.

4.2. Embellishments and Ornamentation: Explore the world of embellishments and ornamentation, adding a touch of opulence to elevate the overall aesthetic.

V. Color Psychology in Shoemaking: Beyond the Surface

Dive into the psychology of color, understanding how color choices can evoke emotions and enhance the visual impact of footwear.

5.1. Classic vs. Contemporary Color Schemes: Analyze the impact of classic and contemporary color schemes, considering cultural influences and fashion trends.

5.2. Personalization through Color: Explore the realm of color personalization, allowing individuals to express their unique style through custom hues.

VI. Texture and Pattern Mastery: Creating Visual Depth

Master the art of incorporating textures and patterns, adding layers of visual interest that elevate the overall appeal of shoes.

6.1. Texture Play in Leathercraft: Examine how various textures in leather contribute to the overall aesthetics, from smooth finishes to textured embossing.

6.2. Intricate Pattern Applications: Unveil the techniques of applying intricate patterns, such as broguing and perforations, that enhance the visual depth of shoes.

VII. Footwear Customization: Tailoring Aesthetics to Individuality

Embrace the era of personalized aesthetics, where shoemakers tailor designs to the unique preferences of individuals.

7.1. Made-to-Order and Bespoke Options: Explore the resurgence of made-to-order and bespoke shoemaking, allowing customers to actively participate in the design process.

7.2. Collaborations with Artisans: Witness the synergy between shoemakers and artisans from other disciplines, creating limited-edition masterpieces that transcend conventional boundaries.

VIII. The Impact of Sustainable Practices: Beauty with a Conscience

Conclude the exploration by recognizing the growing importance of sustainable practices in shoemaking, emphasizing the beauty that arises from ethical choices.

8.1. Eco-Friendly Materials and Processes: Examine the integration of eco-friendly materials and ethical practices, paving the way for a sustainable and visually appealing future.

8.2. Consumer Awareness and Aesthetic Responsibility: Delve into the role of consumers in driving aesthetic responsibility, encouraging sustainable choices in the industry.

AS WE NAVIGATE THE realm of enhancing aesthetic appeal in shoemaking, let us celebrate the union of tradition and innovation, where every stitch tells a story and each design is a testament to the pursuit of visual excellence. "Elevating Excellence: The Art of Enhancing Aesthetic Appeal in Shoemaking" is not just a guide; it's an invitation to appreciate the craftsmanship that transforms footwear into wearable art. May this journey inspire both creators and connoisseurs to revel in the beauty that arises when aesthetics and expertise intertwine.

Chapter 8

Troubleshooting and Quality Control

Common Issues in Shoemaking

Troubleshooting Excellence: Navigating Common Issues in Shoemaking
In the intricate world of shoemaking, where craftsmanship meets precision, a myriad of challenges can arise. From the selection of materials to the final touches, the journey of creating the perfect pair of shoes is not without its hurdles. In this comprehensive exploration, we delve into the common issues faced by shoemakers, offering insights and solutions garnered from the wealth of experience in the art of crafting footwear.

I. INTRODUCTION: THE Pursuit of Perfection
Begin the journey by acknowledging the pursuit of perfection in shoemaking and the inevitability of challenges that accompany this noble craft.
1.1. The Essence of Shoemaking: Set the stage by highlighting the artistry and precision embedded in the process of crafting shoes.
1.2. Acknowledging Challenges: Embrace the reality that challenges are inherent in the pursuit of excellence, shaping the narrative of the shoemaking journey.
II. Material Selection Pitfalls: Navigating the Maze
Explore the pitfalls shoemakers encounter during the material selection process, offering guidance on making informed choices.
2.1. Quality vs. Cost Dilemma: Examine the delicate balance between choosing high-quality materials and managing production costs effectively.

2.2. Understanding Leather Defects: Delve into common leather defects and their impact on the final product, empowering shoemakers to select pristine materials.

III. Design Complications: Balancing Creativity and Practicality

Uncover the complexities of balancing creative designs with the practical aspects of shoemaking, ensuring both aesthetics and functionality.

3.1. Designs vs. Wearability: Navigate the challenges of creating intricate designs while maintaining the wearability and comfort of the finished shoes.

3.2. Ergonomics and Foot Health: Highlight the importance of considering ergonomic factors to address common foot health issues arising from design choices.

IV. Stitching Woes: Ensuring Structural Integrity

Dive into the world of stitching challenges, exploring common issues that impact the structural integrity of the shoe.

4.1. Thread Tension Troubles: Investigate the impact of inconsistent thread tension on the durability and aesthetics of stitched seams.

4.2. Addressing Stitch Misalignment: Provide strategies for overcoming challenges related to stitch misalignment, maintaining precision in every detail.

V. Lasting and Sole Attachment Predicaments: The Foundation Matters

Examine issues related to lasting and sole attachment, emphasizing their pivotal role in the overall construction of a pair of shoes.

5.1. Lasting Imperfections: Shed light on common lasting imperfections and their consequences on the shoe's final form and fit.

5.2. Ensuring Strong Sole Bonds: Address challenges in achieving a secure and durable bond between the sole and the rest of the shoe.

VI. Sizing and Fit Challenges: Crafting for Comfort

Investigate the intricacies of sizing and fit challenges, recognizing their impact on customer satisfaction and overall shoemaking success.

6.1. Navigating Size Discrepancies: Provide solutions for managing size discrepancies and ensuring consistency across different pairs.

6.2. Customization for Optimal Fit: Explore the growing demand for customization to address individual preferences and unique foot shapes.

VII. Finishing Touch Dilemmas: Polishing for Perfection

Conclude the exploration by examining issues related to the final stages of shoemaking, focusing on the finishing touches that elevate the overall quality.

7.1. Polishing Pitfalls: Explore challenges in achieving a flawless polish and maintaining consistent coloring throughout the shoe.

7.2. Quality Control Measures: Introduce effective quality control measures to catch and rectify finishing imperfections before the shoes reach the market.

VIII. The Way Forward: Mastery through Challenges

Reflect on the collective wisdom gained from navigating common issues in shoemaking, emphasizing the mastery that arises from overcoming challenges.

8.1. Continuous Learning: Encourage shoemakers to embrace challenges as opportunities for continuous learning, ultimately refining their craft.

8.2. The Legacy of Resilience: Highlight how resilience in the face of challenges contributes to the legacy of a shoemaker, leaving an indelible mark on the industry.

EMBARK ON THIS JOURNEY through the common issues in shoemaking, where challenges become stepping stones toward mastery. "Troubleshooting Excellence: Navigating Common Issues in Shoemaking" is more than a guide; it's a companion for artisans and enthusiasts alike, fostering a deeper understanding of the art and science behind crafting exceptional footwear. May this exploration empower shoemakers to turn obstacles into opportunities, creating shoes that stand as testaments to their dedication and expertise.

Solutions to Potential Problems

NAVIGATING CHALLENGES: Practical Solutions to Potential Problems in Various Fields

When venturing into any domain, challenges are inevitable. Whether you're a seasoned professional or a newcomer, understanding potential problems and having effective solutions at your disposal is crucial. In this extensive exploration, we delve into a myriad of fields, offering practical solutions to common issues. Our goal is to empower individuals of all backgrounds to overcome obstacles with confidence and expertise.

I. INTRODUCTION: THE Landscape of Challenges

1.1. Embracing the Journey: Acknowledge that challenges are inherent in every field and a fundamental part of the learning and growth process.

1.2. The Importance of Solutions: Highlight the significance of having well-thought-out solutions to navigate potential problems successfully.

II. PERSONAL DEVELOPMENT: A Journey Within

2.1. Overcoming Procrastination: Strategies to conquer procrastination and cultivate habits that drive personal development.

2.2. Building Resilience: Techniques for developing resilience in the face of setbacks, fostering a positive mindset.

2.3. Effective Time Management: Practical approaches to optimize time utilization for enhanced productivity and work-life balance.

III. PROFESSIONAL EXCELLENCE: Thriving in the Workplace

3.1. Conflict Resolution Skills: Insight into resolving workplace conflicts diplomatically, fostering a harmonious environment.

3.2. Effective Communication: Strategies to enhance communication skills, whether in team collaborations or leadership roles.

3.3. Navigating Office Politics: Practical tips to navigate and thrive amidst office politics without compromising integrity.

IV. ENTREPRENEURSHIP: Triumphs Amidst Challenges

4.1. Financial Management: Essential financial strategies for entrepreneurs to ensure the sustainability and growth of their ventures.

4.2. Customer Retention: Approaches to cultivate long-term relationships with customers, ensuring business stability.

4.3. Adapting to Market Trends: Techniques for staying ahead by adapting to evolving market trends and consumer demands.

V. RELATIONSHIPS: NURTURING Bonds and Resolving Conflicts

5.1. Effective Communication in Relationships: Techniques for fostering healthy communication in personal relationships.

5.2. Conflict Resolution in Families: Insight into resolving family conflicts constructively, promoting understanding and unity.

5.3. Navigating Social Circles: Strategies for building meaningful connections and navigating social dynamics gracefully.

VI. HEALTH AND WELLNESS: Holistic Approaches

6.1. Stress Management Techniques: Practical methods to manage stress and maintain mental well-being.

6.2. Balanced Nutrition: Guidelines for achieving a balanced diet to support overall health and vitality.

6.3. Incorporating Exercise Into Daily Life: Strategies for integrating physical activity seamlessly into daily routines.

VII. ACADEMIC EXCELLENCE: Mastering the Learning Journey

7.1. Effective Study Habits: Techniques for optimizing study sessions and retaining information effectively.

7.2. Overcoming Exam Anxiety: Strategies to manage exam-related stress and perform optimally under pressure.

7.3. Choosing a Career Path: Insight into making informed decisions when navigating the path from education to career.

VIII. THE JOURNEY AHEAD: Empowered and Informed

8.1. Continual Growth: Encouragement to view challenges as opportunities for continual growth and improvement.

8.2. Resourcefulness: Emphasis on cultivating a resourceful mindset to tackle future challenges with confidence.

EMBARK ON A JOURNEY of empowerment as we explore solutions to potential problems across diverse realms. "Navigating Challenges: Practical Solutions to Potential Problems in Various Fields" is more than a guide; it's a toolkit for individuals seeking practical wisdom to overcome obstacles and thrive in their personal and professional pursuits. May this exploration be a companion on your journey, offering insights that resonate with your unique experiences and aspirations.

Quality Control Measures

ENSURING EXCELLENCE: A Comprehensive Guide to Quality Control Measures

Quality control is the cornerstone of excellence in any industry, ensuring that products and services meet the highest standards. In this in-depth exploration, we navigate the intricate landscape of quality control measures, providing valuable insights and strategies to guarantee the delivery of exceptional outcomes. Join us on a journey through the principles, methodologies, and best practices that define the world of quality control.

I. INTRODUCTION: THE Essence of Quality Control

1.1. Defining Quality Control: An overview of what quality control entails and its pivotal role in various industries.

1.2. The Importance of Quality Assurance: Highlighting the significance of quality assurance in maintaining customer satisfaction and loyalty.

II. KEY PRINCIPLES of Quality Control

2.1. Customer-Centric Approach: How understanding customer expectations shapes the foundation of effective quality control.

2.2. Continuous Improvement: The philosophy of continual enhancement to adapt to evolving standards and technological advancements.

2.3. Risk Management in Quality Control: Identifying potential risks and implementing preemptive measures to maintain consistent quality.

III. METHODOLOGIES in Quality Control

3.1. Statistical Process Control (SPC): Utilizing statistical methods to monitor and control processes, ensuring they operate efficiently.

3.2. Six Sigma Principles: An exploration of the Six Sigma methodology and its role in minimizing defects and variations.

3.3. Total Quality Management (TQM): Implementing a holistic approach to quality, involving all members of an organization.

IV. QUALITY CONTROL in Manufacturing

4.1. Raw Material Inspection: Strategies for ensuring the quality of raw materials before they enter the production process.

4.2. In-Process Quality Checks: Incorporating checks during manufacturing to identify and rectify defects in real-time.

4.3. Final Product Inspection: Comprehensive inspection protocols for finished products before they reach the market.

V. QUALITY CONTROL in Service Industries

5.1. Customer Service Excellence: How service industries implement quality control in customer interactions.

5.2. Process Efficiency in Services: Applying quality control methodologies to enhance the efficiency of service delivery.

5.3. Quality Metrics in Service Industries: Establishing measurable metrics to evaluate and improve service quality.

VI. REGULATORY COMPLIANCE and Quality Control

6.1. Navigating Regulatory Standards: Understanding and adhering to industry-specific regulations to ensure compliance.

6.2. Documenting Quality Processes: The importance of documentation in demonstrating adherence to regulatory requirements.

6.3. Auditing for Quality: Strategies for internal and external audits to maintain and validate quality control measures.

VII. IMPLEMENTING TECHNOLOGY in Quality Control

7.1. Automation in Quality Assurance: The role of technology, artificial intelligence, and automation in streamlining quality control.

7.2. Data-Driven Decision-Making: Leveraging data analytics for informed quality control decisions and improvements.

7.3. Emerging Technologies in Quality Control: Exploring cutting-edge technologies shaping the future of quality assurance.

VIII. BUILDING A QUALITY Culture

8.1. Leadership's Role in Quality Control: How organizational leaders can foster a culture of quality from top to bottom.

8.2. Employee Training and Engagement: The importance of ongoing training to empower employees as guardians of quality.

8.3. Recognition and Rewards: Acknowledging and rewarding contributions to maintaining high-quality standards.

IX. CONCLUSION: ELEVATING Standards for a Better Tomorrow

9.1. The Continuous Journey of Quality: Emphasizing that quality control is an ongoing process, evolving with industry dynamics.

9.2. The Impact of Quality on Reputation: Reflecting on how a commitment to quality can elevate an organization's reputation.

Embark on a journey through the world of quality control, where excellence is not just a goal but a commitment. "Ensuring Excellence: A Comprehensive Guide to Quality Control Measures" is your companion in navigating the intricacies of maintaining high standards across diverse industries. From principles and methodologies to real-world applications, this guide empowers professionals and enthusiasts alike to champion quality in their respective domains. May this exploration inspire a renewed dedication to excellence and continuous improvement.

Ensuring Every Shoe Meets Standards

ENSURING EVERY SHOE Meets Standards: A Comprehensive Guide to Quality Assurance in Footwear Manufacturing

In the intricate world of footwear manufacturing, the pursuit of excellence is not just a goal; it's a commitment to delivering products that meet the highest standards of quality. "Ensuring Every Shoe Meets Standards" embarks on a journey through the meticulous processes and stringent measures involved in guaranteeing that every pair of shoes surpasses expectations.

I. INTRODUCTION: THE Imperative of Quality Assurance in Shoemaking

1.1. Defining Quality Standards in Footwear: A thorough examination of what constitutes quality in the context of shoemaking.

1.2. The Impact of Quality on Consumer Satisfaction: Illustrating the direct correlation between quality assurance and customer loyalty.

II. KEY COMPONENTS of Shoe Quality Assurance

2.1. Material Selection and Testing: Insights into how the choice of materials profoundly influences the durability and comfort of footwear.

2.2. Craftsmanship Standards: Examining the importance of skilled craftsmanship in ensuring the precision and attention to detail necessary for superior footwear.

2.3. Functional Performance Criteria: Establishing benchmarks for performance, including factors like stability, support, and durability.

III. QUALITY ASSURANCE in Design and Prototyping

3.1. Design Integrity Checks: An exploration of how designs are rigorously assessed to ensure they align with aesthetic and functional standards.

3.2. Prototyping for Perfection: Detailing the iterative process of prototyping, addressing issues early in the development stage.

3.3. User Experience Testing: Incorporating user feedback to refine designs and enhance the overall comfort and usability of the footwear.

IV. MANUFACTURING PROCESSES and Quality Control

4.1. Precision Cutting and Stitching: Delving into the critical stages of production, emphasizing precision cutting techniques and meticulous stitching.

4.2. Lasting and Soling Standards: Ensuring consistency in lasting and soling processes to maintain uniformity across the product line.

4.3. Adhesive and Joining Techniques: Examining the methods employed in joining shoe components for longevity and stability.

V. PERFORMANCE TESTING and Evaluation

5.1. Wear and Tear Analysis: Assessing how shoes withstand various conditions to predict their resilience in real-world scenarios.

5.2. Comfort and Fit Assessment: Using data-driven approaches to measure and enhance comfort, including considerations for different foot shapes and sizes.

5.3. Durability Benchmarking: Establishing benchmarks for the longevity of footwear through comprehensive durability testing.

VI. SUSTAINABILITY and Ethical Considerations in Shoemaking

6.1. Eco-Friendly Materials: A look into the growing trend of using sustainable and environmentally friendly materials in footwear production.

6.2. Ethical Labor Practices: Addressing the importance of fair labor practices and ethical considerations in the manufacturing process.

6.3. Recyclability and End-of-Life Solutions: Exploring approaches to make footwear more recyclable and environmentally responsible.

VII. ADAPTING TO INDUSTRY Trends and Technological Advancements

7.1. Integration of Technology: Assessing the impact of emerging technologies like 3D printing and AI in enhancing quality assurance processes.

7.2. Industry 4.0 in Shoemaking: Embracing the principles of Industry 4.0 to optimize production, reduce errors, and improve overall quality.

7.3. Customization and Personalization: Catering to the growing demand for personalized footwear without compromising on quality.

VIII. REGULATORY COMPLIANCE and Global Standards

8.1. Meeting International Quality Standards: Adhering to global quality benchmarks to ensure that shoes meet regulatory requirements worldwide.

8.2. Certifications and Compliance: Obtaining and maintaining certifications to validate adherence to industry-specific quality standards.

8.3. Risk Mitigation in Shoemaking: Developing strategies to mitigate risks associated with quality issues, including recalls and reputation damage.

IX. CONCLUSION: UPHOLDING Excellence, Step by Step

9.1. The Ongoing Commitment to Quality: Acknowledging that quality assurance is a continuous journey rather than a destination.

9.2. The Future of Footwear Quality Assurance: Anticipating trends and advancements that will shape the future landscape of shoemaking.

Embark on a comprehensive exploration of the rigorous processes, uncompromising standards, and innovative approaches that define quality assurance in the world of shoemaking. "Ensuring Every Shoe Meets Standards" is not just a guide; it's an immersive journey into the heart of an industry dedicated to the pursuit of excellence—one step at a time. Whether you're a seasoned professional or an enthusiast, this guide promises a deeper understanding of the intricate processes that transform raw materials into footwear that stands the test of time. Welcome to the realm where

craftsmanship, precision, and passion converge to ensure that every shoe meets and exceeds the highest standards.

Chapter 9

Exploring Advanced Techniques

Incorporating Unique Design Elements

Incorporating Unique Design Elements: Elevating Footwear Aesthetics with Innovation

In the realm of shoemaking, the marriage of functionality and aesthetics is a delicate dance. "Incorporating Unique Design Elements" delves into the intricate art of transforming footwear into not just a necessity but a statement of individuality and style. This comprehensive guide navigates the labyrinth of creativity, offering insights into the innovative techniques that elevate footwear design to unparalleled heights.

I. INTRODUCTION: THE Fusion of Form and Function

    1.1. Defining Unique Design in Footwear: Exploring the concept of uniqueness in the context of footwear, where each pair tells a distinct story.

    1.2. The Intersection of Aesthetics and Functionality: Understanding how design elements can enhance both the visual appeal and performance of shoes.

II. HISTORICAL INSPIRATIONS and Modern Interpretations

    2.1. Cultural Influences on Design: Tracing the historical roots of footwear design and its evolution across different cultures.

    2.2. Reviving Vintage Styles: Examining how modern shoemakers draw inspiration from historical designs to create contemporary masterpieces.

2.3. The Fusion of Tradition and Innovation: Balancing the timeless with the avant-garde to craft designs that resonate with diverse audiences.

III. MATERIALS AS A Canvas: Exploring Possibilities

3.1. Beyond Leather and Fabric: Investigating unconventional materials that push the boundaries of traditional shoemaking.

3.2. Sustainable Design Practices: Incorporating eco-friendly materials and ethical considerations into the design process.

3.3. The Role of Technology in Material Innovation: Utilizing advancements in material science to create cutting-edge, durable, and stylish footwear.

IV. FROM SKETCH TO Reality: The Design Process Unveiled

4.1. The Art of Sketching: Illuminating the initial stages of bringing a design concept to life through sketches and digital renderings.

4.2. Prototyping and Iterative Design: Navigating the iterative process of refining designs through prototypes and user feedback.

4.3. Collaborations in Design: Exploring how collaborations with artists, influencers, and other industries contribute to unique design outcomes.

V. SIGNATURE STYLES and Brand Identity

5.1. Crafting Iconic Silhouettes: Analyzing how certain brands establish signature styles that become synonymous with their identity.

5.2. Personalization for Individuals: Addressing the growing demand for customized footwear that reflects the uniqueness of each wearer.

5.3. Brand Storytelling through Design: Examining the narrative power of design in conveying the essence and ethos of a brand.

VI. INNOVATIVE DESIGN Techniques

6.1. 3D Printing in Footwear Design: Exploring the revolution brought about by 3D printing technology in creating intricate and personalized designs.

6.2. Embroidery, Embellishments, and Beyond: Delving into traditional and contemporary embellishment techniques that add flair to footwear.

6.3. Integrating Cultural Motifs: Celebrating diversity by incorporating cultural symbols and motifs into designs.

VII. CHALLENGES AND Solutions in Unique Footwear Design

7.1. Balancing Comfort and Aesthetics: Navigating the challenge of creating aesthetically pleasing designs without compromising on comfort.

7.2. Sustainability in Design: Addressing the environmental impact of unique design elements and proposing sustainable solutions.

7.3. Market Trends and Consumer Preferences: Staying attuned to the dynamic landscape of fashion and design preferences.

VIII. THE IMPACT OF Unique Footwear Design on Fashion

8.1. Influence on Runways and Street Style: Tracing the influence of unique footwear designs on high fashion runways and everyday street style.

8.2. Consumer Psychology and Buying Decisions: Understanding how unique designs influence consumer perceptions and purchasing decisions.

8.3. The Ripple Effect on the Industry: Assessing how groundbreaking designs set trends that echo across the entire footwear industry.

IX. CONCLUSION: DESIGNING the Future, Step by Step

9.1. The Endless Quest for Uniqueness: Acknowledging that the journey of unique footwear design is an ongoing exploration.

9.2. Emerging Trends and Future Possibilities: Anticipating the trends and innovations that will shape the future of footwear design.

Embark on a captivating journey through the world of shoemaking, where each step is a brushstroke on the canvas of uniqueness. "Incorporating Unique Design Elements" is not merely a guide; it's an ode to the creative spirit that propels shoemakers to push boundaries and redefine the very essence of footwear. Whether you're a seasoned designer or an enthusiast, this guide promises a profound understanding of the artistry that transforms shoes into wearable masterpieces, each telling a story as unique as the person who wears them. Welcome to a universe where every step is a statement—a testament to the seamless fusion of innovation, aesthetics, and the indomitable spirit of creativity.

Experimental Techniques in Shoemaking

EXPERIMENTAL TECHNIQUES in Shoemaking: Unleashing Creativity in Every Step

In the realm of shoemaking, tradition often meets innovation. "Experimental Techniques in Shoemaking" opens the door to a world where craftsmanship intertwines with cutting-edge methods, resulting in footwear that transcends the ordinary. Let's embark on a journey through the avant-garde, exploring techniques that redefine the very essence of what shoes can be.

I. INTRODUCTION: BREAKING Ground in Footwear Craftsmanship

1.1. Evolution of Shoemaking Techniques: Tracing the historical progression from traditional to experimental methods.

1.2. Defining Experimental Techniques: Exploring what sets experimental shoemaking apart and the impact on design possibilities.

II. MATERIALS BEYOND the Ordinary

2.1. Innovative Leather Treatments: Unveiling experimental processes that transform leather into new textures and colors.

2.2. Sustainable Alternatives: Exploring eco-friendly materials and their integration into experimental shoemaking.

2.3. Synthetic Materials Redefined: Pushing the boundaries of synthetic materials for durability and unique aesthetics.

III. UNCONVENTIONAL Pattern Cutting

3.1. Geometric Precision: Exploring experimental pattern cutting techniques that result in intricate and unconventional shoe designs.

3.2. Adapting to Custom Sizing: How experimental patterns cater to individual feet, breaking away from one-size-fits-all conventions.

IV. 3D PRINTING REVOLUTION

4.1. From Digital Design to Wearable Art: Delving into the transformative power of 3D printing in creating intricate and personalized shoe components.

4.2. Customization Beyond Limits: The role of 3D printing in offering bespoke solutions for personalized and adaptive footwear.

V. INCORPORATING SMART Textiles

5.1. Function Meets Fashion: The integration of smart textiles and how they redefine the purpose of footwear.

5.2. Technological Enhancements: Examining how experimental techniques elevate shoes into wearable tech marvels.

VI. ARTISTIC EMBELLISHMENTS and Surface Treatments

6.1. Beyond Embroidery: Exploring unconventional embellishments like laser-cut designs, metallic accents, and more.

6.2. Experimental Surface Treatments: Techniques that turn shoes into canvases for artistic expression.

VII. HANDCRAFTSMANSHIP Meets Robotics

7.1. The Synergy of Human Touch and Automation: How robotics are integrated into traditional shoemaking processes, enhancing precision and efficiency.

7.2. Maintaining Artisanal Integrity: Balancing the use of technology without compromising the essence of handcrafted quality.

VIII. SUSTAINABLE SHOEMAKING Practices

8.1. Eco-Friendly Dyeing Processes: Innovations in dyeing techniques that minimize environmental impact.

8.2. Biodegradable Components: The rise of experimental materials that contribute to sustainable shoemaking.

IX. CHALLENGES AND Triumphs in Experimental Shoemaking

9.1. Balancing Aesthetics and Functionality: Navigating the fine line between experimental designs and practical, comfortable footwear.

9.2. Market Acceptance and Trends: The reception of experimental footwear in the fashion industry and its influence on trends.

X. FUTURE HORIZONS: What Lies Ahead

10.1. Technological Advancements: Anticipating how future technologies will further shape the landscape of experimental shoemaking.

10.2. Collaborations and Cross-Industry Influence: Exploring how partnerships with other industries contribute to avant-garde shoemaking.

Embark on a thrilling exploration of experimental shoemaking, where every pair becomes a testament to innovation, creativity, and a commitment to pushing boundaries. "Experimental Techniques in Shoemaking" is not just a book; it's an invitation to witness the convergence of tradition and futuristic vision. Whether you're a seasoned shoemaker, a design enthusiast, or someone seeking insight into the evolution of footwear, this guide promises a captivating journey through the uncharted territories of experimental shoemaking. Welcome to a world where every step is an expression, and every shoe is a work of art in motion.

Pushing the Boundaries of Innovation

PUSHING THE BOUNDARIES of Innovation in Modern Industry

Innovation is the heartbeat of progress, the driving force that propels industries forward into uncharted territories. In the fast-paced landscape of modern business, staying ahead requires not just keeping pace with change but actively pushing the boundaries of what's possible. This exploration delves into the multifaceted realm of innovation, dissecting its core principles, examining its application across diverse sectors, and anticipating the future landscape shaped by relentless creativity.

I. INTRODUCTION TO Innovation: Unveiling the Essence

1.1. Defining Innovation: A comprehensive exploration of what innovation truly entails and its role in shaping industries.

1.2. The Evolution of Innovation: Tracing the historical trajectory of innovation and its transformative impact on societies.

II. THE PILLARS OF Innovative Thinking

2.1. Cultivating a Culture of Innovation: How organizations foster an environment that encourages and nurtures creative thinking.

2.2. Innovative Leadership: The pivotal role leaders play in driving a culture of continuous improvement and risk-taking.

III. DISRUPTIVE TECHNOLOGIES: A Paradigm Shift

3.1. Artificial Intelligence and Machine Learning: The transformative power of AI and ML in reshaping industries.

3.2. Blockchain Revolution: Unraveling the impact of blockchain beyond cryptocurrency, transforming processes and systems.

IV. INDUSTRY CASE STUDIES: Innovations in Action

4.1. Tech Giants' Paradigm Shifts: Examining how companies like Apple, Google, and Tesla have redefined innovation within their sectors.

4.2. Biotech Innovations: Pioneering advancements in biotechnology that revolutionize healthcare, agriculture, and beyond.

V. SUSTAINABLE INNOVATION: Balancing Progress and Responsibility

5.1. Green Technologies: Innovations fostering sustainability in energy, transportation, and manufacturing.

5.2. Circular Economy Initiatives: How industries are rethinking product lifecycles for a more sustainable future.

VI. THE HUMAN FACTOR in Innovation

6.1. Innovative Workspaces: Redefining office environments to stimulate creativity and collaboration.

6.2. Innovation in Human Resources: Transformative approaches to talent acquisition, development, and retention.

VII. CHALLENGES AND Risks: Navigating the Innovation Landscape

7.1. Balancing Risk and Reward: The delicate equilibrium organizations must maintain when embracing innovative strategies.

7.2. Ethical Considerations: Addressing the ethical dilemmas posed by cutting-edge technologies and practices.

VIII. THE GLOBAL INNOVATION Ecosystem

8.1. International Collaboration: How countries collaborate to drive global innovation, sharing knowledge and resources.

8.2. Innovation Hubs: Spotlighting the epicenters of innovation worldwide and their contributions to progress.

IX. FUTURE FRONTIERS: A Glimpse into Tomorrow

9.1. Emerging Technologies: Anticipating the game-changers that will define the next era of innovation.

9.2. Interdisciplinary Innovation: The fusion of technologies and industries creating unforeseen possibilities.

X. CONCLUSION: INSPIRING the Next Wave of Innovators

10.1. Empowering the Next Generation: Strategies for fostering innovation in education and inspiring future innovators.

10.2. Sustaining the Momentum: How industries can maintain their innovative edge in an ever-evolving world.

Innovation isn't a solitary pursuit; it's a collective force that shapes the future. "Pushing the Boundaries of Innovation in Modern Industry" is not just a documentation of progress; it's an invitation to envision the limitless potential that unfolds when creativity meets determination. Whether you're an entrepreneur, a business leader, or an enthusiast of the ever-evolving landscape of innovation, this exploration promises an insightful journey into the heart of transformative change. Welcome to a world where each idea is a spark, and each innovation is a step into the uncharted territories of possibility.

Future Trends in Shoemaking

FUTURE TRENDS IN SHOEMAKING: A Glimpse into Footwear Innovation

In the dynamic realm of shoemaking, the horizon is perpetually marked by innovation and evolution. The amalgamation of traditional craftsmanship and cutting-edge technology creates a fertile ground for future trends that promise not just style but also functionality and sustainability. This exploration delves into the anticipated trends that will redefine the landscape of shoemaking in the years to come.

I. INTRODUCTION: THE Ever-Evolving World of Footwear

1.1. Shoemaking Through Time: A brief historical overview of the evolution of shoemaking techniques.

1.2. Current State of the Industry: A snapshot of the contemporary shoemaking landscape, highlighting recent innovations.

II. SUSTAINABLE MATERIALS and Practices

2.1. Eco-Friendly Materials: The rise of sustainable alternatives like recycled fabrics, bio-based leathers, and plant-derived materials.

2.2. Circular Design Principles: Embracing circular economy models to reduce waste and extend the lifecycle of footwear.

III. CUSTOMIZATION and Personalization

3.1. 3D Printing in Shoemaking: How 3D printing technology is revolutionizing the creation of custom-fit footwear.

3.2. Individualized Design: The trend towards personalized shoe designs to cater to unique preferences and needs.

IV. SMART AND CONNECTED Footwear

4.1. Integration of Technology: Incorporating smart features like fitness tracking, temperature control, and adaptive cushioning.

4.2. Connected Footwear Ecosystem: The role of shoes in the broader context of the Internet of Things (IoT).

V. ARTISANAL CRAFTSMANSHIP in the Digital Age

5.1. Digital Tools for Artisans: How technology aids traditional craftsmen in enhancing precision and efficiency.

5.2. Preserving Heritage Techniques: Balancing innovation with the preservation of time-honored craftsmanship.

VI. FUTURISTIC MATERIALS and Designs

6.1. Nanomaterials in Footwear: The application of nanotechnology for enhanced durability, flexibility, and performance.

6.2. Architectural and Avant-Garde Designs: Exploring unconventional structures and futuristic aesthetics.

VII. FOOTWEAR FOR HEALTH and Wellness

7.1. Biomechanics in Design: Designing shoes that promote foot health and overall well-being.

7.2. Recovery and Performance Enhancement: Footwear innovations for athletes and those seeking enhanced physical performance.

VIII. GLOBAL INFLUENCES on Shoemaking Trends

8.1. Cultural Fusion: How diverse cultural influences shape the design and style of contemporary footwear.

8.2. Global Collaborations: Collaborative efforts that transcend borders to create unique and inclusive footwear.

IX. CHALLENGES AND Opportunities in the Future Landscape

9.1. Sustainability Challenges: Addressing the environmental impact of mass production and consumption.

9.2. Ethical Considerations: Navigating the ethical implications of technological advancements in shoemaking.

X. CONCLUSION: STEPPING into Tomorrow

10.1. The Ever-Changing Canvas of Shoemaking: Embracing a future where each step is a testament to innovation.

10.2. A Call to Creativity: Encouraging designers, manufacturers, and enthusiasts to actively contribute to shaping the future of footwear.

IN THE FAST-PACED WORLD of shoemaking, the journey towards the future is marked by a delicate dance between tradition and innovation. "Future Trends in Shoemaking" is not merely a forecast; it's an invitation to partake in the exciting narrative of an industry that continually pushes the boundaries of what is possible. Whether you're an avid follower of fashion, an aspiring designer, or simply someone with an appreciation for comfortable and stylish footwear, this exploration promises a captivating glimpse into the future that awaits beneath our feet. Step into the world of tomorrow, where every shoe is a story waiting to be told.

Conclusion

Conclusion: Paving the Path Forward in Shoemaking

In concluding our exploration into the intricate world of shoemaking, we find ourselves standing at the intersection of tradition and innovation. The journey through various facets of this craft—from precision cutting techniques to futuristic materials—reveals a dynamic landscape that mirrors the diversity of human expression and functionality.

I. BRIDGING CRAFTSMANSHIP with Innovation

As we wrap our discussion, it's paramount to acknowledge the seamless integration of craftsmanship with cutting-edge innovation. Traditional techniques, refined over centuries, are now complemented by advanced technologies, paving the way for a new era in shoemaking. The delicate dance between the old and the new is not a struggle for dominance but a harmonious collaboration that enriches the industry.

II. EMBRACING SUSTAINABLE Practices

The future of shoemaking is intrinsically tied to sustainability. Our exploration uncovered the rise of eco-friendly materials, circular design principles, and a collective commitment to reducing the environmental footprint. Embracing sustainability is not just a trend; it's a responsibility to ensure that the beauty and functionality of footwear leave a positive, lasting impact.

III. A SYMPHONY OF Design and Comfort

The customization and personalization trends underscore a fundamental shift towards prioritizing individual preferences and needs. Whether through 3D printing for bespoke designs or the integration of smart features, the emphasis is on providing unparalleled comfort without compromising on style. Shoes are not merely accessories; they are extensions of one's identity and lifestyle.

IV. NAVIGATING CHALLENGES, Seizing Opportunities

While the shoemaking landscape is rife with innovation, it is not without its challenges. The delicate balance between tradition and modernity, the ethical considerations of technological advancements, and the imperative to address sustainability challenges are aspects that demand careful navigation. However, within these challenges lie opportunities for growth, learning, and transformative change.

V. STEPPING INTO TOMORROW

As we step into the future, the shoemaking industry invites us to be active participants in its evolution. The experimental techniques, futuristic designs, and global influences underscore a narrative that is not confined to a single perspective. Each shoe tells a story, and collectively, they narrate the tale of an industry that continues to push the boundaries of what is possible.

VI. A CALL TO THE SHOEMAKING Community

To the shoemakers, designers, manufacturers, and enthusiasts who breathe life into this industry, the journey does not end here. It is an ongoing narrative, a story waiting to be written with every cut, stitch, and innovation. As we forge ahead, let us embrace the challenges, celebrate the triumphs, and collectively shape a future where shoemaking is an artistry that resonates with the soul.

IN CONCLUSION, THE world of shoemaking is a captivating fusion of art and science, tradition and innovation. It's a journey where each step leaves an indelible mark on the canvas of fashion and function. As we bid farewell to this exploration, we carry with us the understanding that every pair of shoes is more than just a product—it's a testament to human creativity, resilience, and the relentless pursuit of excellence in craftsmanship. Here's to the future of shoemaking, where every shoe tells a story, and every story is a step towards a more vibrant, sustainable, and stylish world.

www.ingramcontent.com/pod-product-compliance
Lightning Source LLC
LaVergne TN
LVHW051703050326
832903LV00032B/3976

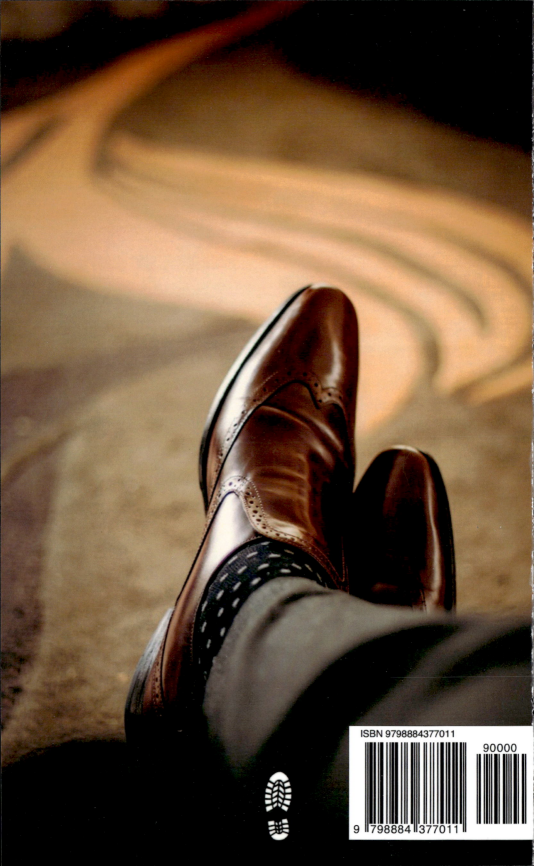

ISBN 9798884377011

90000